Splendors of Godly Love

Splendors of Godly Love

Chris N. van der Merwe

Foreword by Chris Jones

WIPF & STOCK · Eugene, Oregon

SPLENDORS OF GODLY LOVE

Copyright © 2017 Chris N. van der Merwe. All rights reserved. Except for brief quotations in critical publications or reviews, no part of this book may be reproduced in any manner without prior written permission from the publisher. Write: Permissions, Wipf and Stock Publishers, 199 W. 8th Ave., Suite 3, Eugene, OR 97401.

Wipf & Stock
An Imprint of Wipf and Stock Publishers
199 W. 8th Ave., Suite 3
Eugene, OR 97401

www.wipfandstock.com

PAPERBACK ISBN: 978-1-5326-1760-7
HARDCOVER ISBN: 978-1-4982-4241-7
EBOOK ISBN: 978-1-4982-4240-0

Manufactured in the U.S.A.   JULY 25, 2017

For Biebie

Contents

Foreword by Chris Jones | *ix*
Introduction | *xi*

1   Faith | 1
2   Hope | 21
3   Righteousness Etc. | 39
4   Humility | 60
5   Joy and Peace | 78
6   Truth | 95
7   Love | 110

Bibliography | *127*

Foreword

SPLENDORS OF GODLY LOVE is a unique and timely book for this age in which many of us worry about the fragility of the moral fiber of our society. While reflecting on some of the values taught in the Gospels, the author argues that we need more than a constitution, human rights, or democratic ideals to establish a truly moral community.

Chris van der Merwe digs deep into the Word and combines biblical treasures with beautiful stories and appropriate literary quotes. This splendid book on godly love focusses on several values to guide us in the many decisions, opportunities, and temptations in our lives.

Our world is deeply troubled by moral confusion. In the depths of many people's mind, there is an emptiness—which cannot be filled by money. Although many people place very high value on material wealth, we need a "currency" of a different kind.

This book helps us to rethink not only the biblical values addressed in it, but to rediscover the meaning of life and our place in the world. It wants to strengthen us in the volatility and trauma of our earthly existence.

The French novelist Marcel Proust once said, "The real voyage of discovery consists not in seeking new lands, but in seeing with new eyes." Much of what should happen in this world lies in the minds of people. This book wants to renew minds with the wonderful gift of love, because eyes are useless in the voyage of discovery where the mind is blind to godly love.

Foreword

As a literary scholar, Chris is a fine observer and communicates his insights with great clarity. With his ear to the ground, and his heart close to the gospel, he brings together the social context of the twenty-first century and the ancient values of the Gospels in a beautiful and creative way.

It is a practical and digestible book which is not written in a religious language that only speaks to one's private life. The author makes the gospel clearly relevant to the search for a just and humane society.

Splendors of Godly Love is not a book to be tossed aside lightly. It should, so to speak, be "sown" with great urgency among the people "out there" so that they can read it and apply this treasury of truths to their lives in order to experience joy and peace, justice, hope, humility, truth and faith—all related to love.

This challenging, inspiring, and healing book is highly recommended!

Chris Jones
Director of the Center for Morality and Moral Leadership
University of Stellenbosch

Introduction

KNOWINGLY OR UNKNOWINGLY, WE are all searching for values. We are forced to make decisions every day, and our choices are based on our sense of values. In a world that is becoming more and more materialistic, material wealth is increasingly seen as the supreme value to strive for. And yet, material wealth has its limitations; there is an emptiness deep inside us that money cannot fill.

The Bible writes about values of a moral nature, to guide us in our daily living with its many choices, opportunities, and temptations. They are values that give meaning to our lives; they last through the ups and downs of our earthly existence, and even beyond. The values that I will be discussing in the following chapters are: faith, hope, righteousness, truth, joy, humility, and love. They seem to be such familiar, well-worn concepts that we tend not to expect much of them in our modern days. They were meant for more primitive times, we imagine. And yet, how often these virtues are misunderstood; we have to rethink them and rediscover their significance in a world troubled by meaninglessness and moral confusion. We have to examine the life and teachings of Jesus anew to discover the richness of their content and their relevance to our times. We have to cleanse them from the layers of dirt accumulated through centuries of distortion.

The seven concepts dealt with in the following chapters are not to be confused with the traditional seven cardinal virtues as opposed to the seven deadly sins. The choice of topics is in some way subjective—the virtues are those which, to my mind, are most closely connected to the central Christian value of love, which has gripped and challenged me all my life. The God of the Christians is a God of love, and the core of God's commandments is the law of love—but what does the many-splendored concept of love entail? The book was written as a response to this all-important question.

The concepts of faith, hope, righteousness, truth, humility, joy, and love are linked; they all give us a glimpse of the glorious nature of God as revealed in Jesus, the incarnate Word of God, and of the way God wants us to lead our lives. The search for the meaning of love and its relevance for our daily lives is essentially a search to know more about the God of love, and it springs from the desire to reflect something of God's splendor in our daily lives. In such a way, and such a way only, our empty lives can be filled with meaning.

I do not, in the following chapters, delve into theological controversies. I have been trained in literary analysis, not in theology, and I will carefully analyze relevant biblical texts handed down by successive generations of Christians and explore the richness and relevance of their content, in an attempt to come nearer to understanding the God in whom I trust.

1

Faith

A Principal Virtue

The New Testament makes a surprisingly big issue of the virtue of faith. For instance, Jesus asks blind men about their belief in him before healing them, and afterwards he tells them that they were healed "according to [their] faith" (Matt 9:28).[1] He even says to the woman who suffered from hemorrhages: "Your faith has made you well" (Luke 8:48). In contrast, he could perform no "deeds of power" among the people of Nazareth, "because of their unbelief" (Matt 13:58). In the letters of Paul, too, the importance of believing is stressed. In his letter to the Romans he reminds his readers that the great founder of the nation of Israel, the patriarch Abraham, pleased God not by what he did, but because he "believed God" (Rom 4:3). "No distrust made him waver" (Rom 4:20). Similarly, we have to have faith to be justified by God (Rom 1:17).

This importance attached to believing seems strange to us. Believing or not believing, we think, lies outside the sphere of virtue. Normally we can check the facts when a statement is made and decide to believe or not to believe accordingly. For instance, if someone says it is raining, we can look outside and see whether it is true—no merit in that. We can believe Einstein's theory of relativity, on the authority of experts, even though the theory contains

---

1. All biblical quotations are from the New Revised Standard Version.

some notions incomprehensible to us—but the virtue lies more with Einstein than with us who believe on the authority of experts without being able to comprehend Einstein's ideas. On the other hand, if someone believes the earth is flat, we may find him somewhat odd, but not therefore deserving eternal damnation. More important to us, from an ethical point of view, is the question of whether a person is kind and generous. Clearly, the biblical faith must entail more than a mere rational belief in empirical facts.

Karen Armstrong points in the right direction when she reminds us that "the word translated *faith* in the New Testament is the Greek *pistis* (verbal form *pisteuo*) which means trust; loyalty; engagement; commitment."[2] The concept contains much more than rational belief. Let us then consider the meaning of faith in the biblical sense.

Champions of Faith

In Hebrews 11:1 we have a definition of faith, but it leaves many questions unanswered: "Now faith is the assurance of things hoped for, the conviction of things not seen." To be certain of the things you are hoping for is an example of circular reasoning—you must hope what you believe, and believe what you hope; but what is the ground for hoping and believing? In our daily lives, our certainties are to a large extent based on what we can observe through the senses: we believe what we have seen. But this text turns any assumption we have on its head: it encourages us to believe what we have not seen. We tend to say: "Seeing is believing," but the text implies that believing is seeing—first believe, then you will see.

The rest of the chapter provides us with historical examples of people who were rewarded for their actions based on faith. Two of the most interesting examples are Noah and Abraham. Noah built a ship on dry ground in anticipation of the flood promised by God; Abraham became the father of Isaac when Sarah was past childbearing age. When God demanded it, Abraham was even

---

2. Armstrong, *Case for God*, 90.

willing to sacrifice the son whom he had so miraculously received. In both instances, faith was rewarded in a tangible way. Noah was vindicated when the flood came and was saved by the ark that he built. Abraham received the promised son, and got him back when he showed his willingness to sacrifice Isaac to God.

The people of their time must have thought these two champions of faith quite crazy. To build an ark on dry ground must have seemed madness; and to expect your wife to fall pregnant when she does not menstruate anymore, and when the time to "have pleasure" is over, was more than slightly odd (Gen 18:11–12). The heroes of faith were people who went against the dictates of "common sense"; they were rewarded for swimming against the current.

Abraham and Noah could subsequently see the reward for their faith; but faith does not always bring such tangible results—not in one's own lifetime, anyway. Some of God's promises to Abraham were fulfilled before his death; others were not. He died as a stranger in Canaan—God's promise that his descendants would inherit the land still lay in the distant future. Moses, who also persevered unflinchingly on the road of faith, "as though he saw Him who is invisible" (Heb 11:27), was not allowed to reach the goal of his journey: he died with the promised land still beckoning in the distance. A number of saints, martyred for their faithfulness, "did not receive what was promised" (Heb 11:39)—their lives ended in expectation of what was to come. And the prophet Jeremiah, as a theologian once remarked, died with so many unfulfilled prophecies on his hands. It's not so easy to believe when you cannot see.

Kinds of Faith

We should distinguish between three different kinds of faith: (a) the secular meaning of faith, (b) faith to be healed, and (c) faith to be saved. I will use the words "faith," "belief," and "trust" alternately, for the meanings of these words overlap—they all have to do with accepting the truth of that which cannot be seen. But we should also remember that they have different connotations. "Belief" is often regarded as an acceptance of the mind, whereas the biblical faith contains an element of trust—a risk is involved; there is more at stake than mere intellectual acceptance.

(a) All people use some kind of faith every day. Faith is not irrational; it is essential: we have to believe in order to live. The choice is not between believing and not believing; the choice is what to believe in. We trust our senses, and don't cross the street when a car is approaching. We board an airplane because we believe it will go to the destination promised by the airline. We believe in maps and in news reports—it is impossible to check all the information that we take for granted.

Natural scientists, doing their experiments, trust their senses and their logic. They also trust the objects being examined, that they won't have completely different qualities in future. They have a belief in the orderliness of the universe. Many scientists have also acknowledged the belief in beauty as a guiding principle in their search for understanding the universe, and their intuitive belief has repeatedly been confirmed by the results. They have presumed the invisible.

In the business world no enterprise would be started without some faith in the future; it may later be proved wrong, but the point is that nothing will happen without the faith that the venture could succeed. No marriage could be happy without faith in the partner. The faith could prove to be misguided and the marriage could fail, but without trust it has no chance at all. Worthwhile enterprises are based on faith: people believe in the workability of an ideal and act on that assumption to realize their dream—they take the risk involved in their faith. A world without any form of faith would be a world without any kind of action. A world without any predictability would be a nightmare, impossible to live in.

(b) As mentioned before, Jesus required that people who approached him to be healed believe in him before he performed the healing. That's strange—why not heal them first, so that they could learn to believe in his power? The kind of faith that Jesus required, however, was more than a faith based on observation; he expected them to trust in him. He wanted them to acknowledge something even more important than being healed—to know who he was:

the Son of God, the incarnation of God's empathy and power. He wished them to enter into a personal relationship with him, honoring him as the Messiah sent by God. The healing of the body had to be coupled with the healing of the soul. Furthermore, he wanted to teach them that faith is not merely based on facts, but that facts can be changed through faith. He encouraged people to participate, through their faith, in the miracle he performed, to become partners in the process of healing.

(c) The faith that is such a central theme in the writing of Paul is the faith needed to be justified before God and to be saved from the slavery of sin. It is a faith that realizes our inadequacy to obtain the righteousness that God requires, our inability to transform our lives according to the standards of God. Jesus, through his selfless sacrifice, his courage, his caring love, and his faithfulness unto death, set a standard that we can never hope to reach. If Jesus was merely an example, sent to teach us how to live, then his coming to the earth is bad news indeed. He raised the standards and made the goal unattainable.

But the Gospels are narratives of good news. When Jesus established the sacrament of Holy Communion, he indicated that his glory can be passed on to us through our identification with his sacrifice. Just as we stay alive physically by eating and drinking, we can become alive spiritually, free from the bondage of guilt and sin, by partaking in faith of the bread and wine symbolizing the body and blood of Christ. The Gospels bring us good news with the bad news—the bad news is that we cannot save ourselves; the good news is that there is a way of salvation.

The salvation of Christ does not provide us with a cheap forgiveness of sins, allowing us to do exactly what we want once our sins have been forgiven. Holy Communion, when performed as an act of faith, of identification with the crucified and risen Christ, cannot leave us unchanged. It requires a kind of daily death and resurrection: a "death" of the flesh, of our natural pride and stubbornness, our insistence to control our own lives. And it opens up a new life of harmony with our God, with ourselves, and with our fellows—liberated from our inner discord. Bit by bit we are transformed unto the likeness of Jesus, reflecting his loving care, his total obedience to God.

These then, are three forms of faith that we can distinguish. Obviously, the second and third forms of faith are the ones that are most relevant here. I said that the Bible brings good news with the "bad news." With the offer of salvation comes a stern command: to be loving towards all people as Jesus was, and to obey God unreservedly as he did. The biblical salvation is totally free, and yet extremely costly: it is granted without merit, through faith, but it costs everything, a total surrender of our lives to the will of God.

Rational Grounds for the Leap of Faith

In an age where we all love to be in control of our own lives, and even to control other people's lives, it is no wonder that we are hesitant to take the biblical leap of faith. Truth is, we normally need a hard push before we are willing to take it. The "push" can take on a variety of forms: we can be exasperated by our lives falling apart, worn down by our feelings of guilt, anxious about the emptiness of our existence, troubled by illness, or scared by death. At our wits' end, we might be persuaded to take a leap—a leap that could transform our lives. Our sins could be forgiven, our lives filled with meaning, and death could lose its threat.

The leap of faith is not completely rational, as we have seen; but is also not irrational. Just as we accept the authority of many sources of information in our daily, secular lives, so we can also trust the authority of the witnesses of the life of Jesus. At the beginning of the first letter of John the writer emphasizes that he knows what he is talking about: he writes about "what we have heard, what we have seen with our eyes, what we have looked at and touched with our hands, concerning the word of life . . . we declare to you what we have seen and heard" (1 John 1:1, 3). Every day we trust our own senses; the writer urges his readers also to trust the senses of the apostles who observed the life, death, and resurrection of Jesus from close quarters.

The reliability of the apostles to act as witnesses is based not only on their personal observations but also on their subsequent behavior. The apostles proved the integrity of their faith by their willingness to sacrifice their lives for the truth of what they believed. They were beaten, put in jail, banned, tortured, and killed; but they stuck to their belief in Jesus as Savior, as the one who conquered sin and death. Many people have expressed their doubts as to whether Jesus "really" rose from the dead, and that is understandable, for it is difficult for modern people to believe in miracles; but it is hard to deny that the disciples of Jesus were convinced of his resurrection, that they saw it as proof that God anointed him as the Messiah to save the world. These martyrs are witnesses who claim to be worthy of our trust.

There is another ground for John's belief—he mentions it in the same chapter: "Truly our fellowship is with the Father and with his Son Jesus Christ" (1 John 1:3). John's faith is based not only on the past, but on the present—on the presence of the Father and the Son with him and in him. His faith is fed daily by faithfulness to God—he knows that there is no such thing as faith from a distance. It is worthy to note that the faith of many people weakens and dies, not through new, reliable evidence presented to them, but through a fading of their faithfulness. It is like someone taking leave of a friend before going to stay elsewhere. At first she writes to or phones the friend, but then the letters, the emails, and the conversations get fewer and fewer, and ultimately stop altogether. Finally, she could not tell whether the friend is dead or alive. In such a way God "dies" in many people's lives.

Faith and Will

There is a strong connection between faith and will. The Gospel of Mark tells the story of the paralytic whose friends brought him to Jesus to be healed. When they could not reach Jesus because such a huge crowd was gathered around him, they removed the roof of the house where Jesus was and, "having dug through it, they let down the mat on which the paralytic lay" (Mark 2:4). Their audacity possibly gave the owner of the house a fit, but Jesus was clearly impressed by their behavior: "When Jesus saw their faith, he said to the paralytic, 'Son, your sins are forgiven'" (2:5). Apart from the fact that we see an example here of what was mentioned before—that Jesus linked the healing of the body to the healing of the soul—we note another relevant point: Jesus appreciated all the trouble that the friends of the paralytic took to help him; he was impressed by the care for their friend and their determination to have him healed. Such a strong-willed faith, their eyes unwaveringly fixed on their goal, not stopped by any obstacles—such is the faith appreciated by Jesus.

Often we make all kinds of excuses for not believing, but we hide our real reason—our unwillingness to lead a life of faith. A. N. Wilson, author of a biography of C. S. Lewis as well as a quite unconventional biography of Jesus, wrote an article in the *Daily Mail*. In the article he analyses his turn to atheism and his subsequent reconversion to Christianity. The underlying motives for his adherence to atheism are candidly confessed:

> Why did I, along with so many others, become so dismissive of Christianity?
>
> Like most educated people in Britain and Northern Europe (I was born in 1950), I have grown up in a culture that is overwhelmingly secular and anti-religious. The universities, broadcasters and media generally are not merely non-religious, they are positively anti.
>
> To my shame, I believe it was this that made me lose faith and heart in my youth. It felt so uncool to be religious. With the mentality of a child in the playground, I felt at some visceral level that being religious was unsexy, like having spots or wearing specs.[3]

The real point of entrance into a life of faith lies at the will—what is needed is a willingness to bow before the will of God, to admit our inability to save ourselves and to accept God's salvation. Faith is therefore closely connected to humility; we have to acknowledge our need of God. The proud person cannot possibly admit his

---

3. Wilson, "Religion of Hatred."

brokenness or bow his knees before the Almighty. "I'm the greatest!" says the proud one; "God's the greatest!" says the believer. In the parable of the Pharisee and the tax collector, the Pharisee thanks God that he is better than others, while the tax collector pleads for God to be merciful upon him, a sinner. Jesus concludes by saying that the tax collector rather than the Pharisee was justified by God . . . for all who exalt themselves will be humbled, but all who humble themselves will be exalted" (Luke 18:14).

Doubting Believers

The grace of God—that we are saved not by good works, but by believing in Christ—is at the heart of Christianity. The point that we are saved by faith can, however, easily lead people to think that they are saved not by Christ, but by their own faith. They emphasize their faith, not Christ's grace; faith becomes a good work for them, an achievement, and an outlet for their suppressed pride. The real message of the gospel is different.

In the Gospel of Mark the story is told of a boy suffering from fits whose father brought him to Jesus to be healed. The reply of Jesus is typical: "All things can be done for the one who believes" (Mark 9:23). Jesus makes the remark to test the father, and the father immediately realizes that he has a problem to pass the test, for his faith is not perfect. But just like the friends of the paralyzed man who brought him to Jesus, the father is desperate for Jesus' help, and cries out in anguish: "I believe; help my unbelief" (9:24). The father must have heard a lot about the healing power of Jesus; he must have had some ground for saying: "I believe." He clearly feels exasperated by his incomplete faith—some translations add that he cries out "with tears." The father wants to believe, but cannot completely; and Jesus extends his grace to him. The mercy of Jesus is sufficient for our half-hearted belief—even for our half-hearted will. Although he will never force his will upon us, he will help our weak wills and our doubting hearts, as long as we want to will and to believe. Our inadequacy does not extinguish his grace, but stimulates it.

Faith is pleasing to God; but there is also a kind of doubt, an honest doubt, that is pleasing to God. We find an example of that in the book of Job. A number of calamities strike him and his family, and Job, a devout man, understandably questions the righteousness of God. Why is it that a good man suffers and evil men prosper? His friends, who come to console him, plead the case of God; they assure Job that somewhere he must have done something wrong, for God can never be unjust. Neither Job nor his friends are allowed into the mystery of God's reason for God's actions, but Job receives a marvelous encouragement at the end of the story. With the following words God turns to Eliphaz, one of the three men who argued with Job: "My wrath is kindled against you and against your two friends; for you have not spoken of me what is right, as my servant Job has" (Job 42:7). God prefers the person who asks sincere questions and expresses honest doubt to those who utter conventional "pious" words without any insight.

Faith and Good Works

There is an age-old debate among Christians about the relationship between faith and good works. However, the opposition between faith and works is a false opposition; they are two sides of the same coin. Paul stresses that we are saved by faith and faith alone, without any merit on our part; James, on the other hand, emphasizes the importance of good works. He states: "Just as the body without the spirit is dead, so faith without works is also dead" (Jas 2:26). Paul uses the example of Abraham to show that the latter was justified by faith; James points out that Abraham's faith went over into action, and that he was justified by his deeds (Jas 2:21–22). Rahab the prostitute, one of the champions of faith mentioned in Hebrews 11, welcomed the spies of Israel into Jericho. James uses her as an example to show the importance of deeds. And indeed, if one examines the lives of the heroes of faith discussed in Hebrews 11, it becomes clear that in all these cases faith was combined with action. It is indeed as James writes: faith and works go together, and the one without the other is dead.

One should also remember that the motive for a Christian's good deeds is not to win God's favor or to impress the world. Christian good works are done out of gratitude to God and care for others. The sequence is different from what the world would expect: we are first saved without good deeds, but subsequently good deeds flow from our salvation. Yet that is not the whole truth. Good works do not begin after conversion, and faith does not stop there. Is there not something good in the act of conversion itself, when one decides to trust God and surrender oneself to God? And on the other hand, are our good deeds not done in faith, in humble dependence on God's guidance and grace?

Indeed; inextricably interwoven, from beginning to end in the Christian's life, are a total dependence on God and complete trust in God, on the one hand, and on the other hand, an active response to God's grace and a willing involvement in virtuous deeds to which God calls us. To use an image of C. S. Lewis: it's like the two blades of a pair of scissors; one can never say which of the two blades did the cutting. The Christian life is like the running of a marathon: a combination of own effort and help from outside. At the end one could say: "Wow, but I ran well! I didn't succumb to my tiredness. I continued to breathe deeply and rhythmically, my legs carried me forward, I persevered to the end." Or one could say: "Was it not for the food I had before the start of the race, for the assistance and drinks I received along the way, for the air I breathed from moment to moment, I would have been lost. Even my body is not my own; in the womb I was conceived, in no ways am I a self-made person." And both remarks would be true. All the effort would have been worthless without the grace of food, drink, and air, and of life itself, but grace would have been useless without one's own effort.

Faith and Trust in Human Beings

So far we have only looked at faith as a matter between God and us. There is another aspect of the theme: faith in our fellow human beings. Such a faith does not focus exclusively on other people's shortcomings, but notes their good points as well, as ground for faith in them; it is conscious of their potential. Faith in God and faith in our fellow human beings go together, for we should not primarily have faith in others because we believe in their trustworthiness, but because we believe in the Creator in whose image all people were created, and in the Spirit of God working in their lives.

Jesus gave us a wonderful example of interpersonal faith in his relationship with Peter. Choosing Peter, not only to be one of his disciples, but to be their leader, was a rather strange choice. So often Peter misunderstood the message of Jesus. For instance, when Jesus talks about his coming death, Peter regards it his duty to reprimand him, so that Jesus has to answer quite severely: "Get behind me, Satan! You are a stumbling-block to me; for you are setting your mind not on divine things but on human things" (Matt 16:23).

Thus we see that Jesus' faith in Peter is not one that is blind to his faults; but Jesus knows that there is more to Peter than his weaknesses. Indeed, Peter has some bright moments where he shows insight into the true nature and calling of Jesus. When Jesus questions the disciples about his identity, Peter answers: "You are the Messiah, the Son of the living God" (Matt 16:16). Jesus responds by praising him and telling him what a special place he would have in the coming kingdom: "And I tell you, you are Peter, and on this rock I will build my church. . . . I will give you the keys of the kingdom of heaven, and whatever you bind on earth will be bound in heaven, and whatever you loose on earth will be loosed in heaven" (16:18–19).

Jesus changes from calling him "Simon son of Jonah" to "Peter," that is, "the rock" (16:17–18). The new name indicates a change of direction and a change of identity for the disciple. Jesus believes that Simon will develop into Peter, not because of Simon's own abilities in the first place, but because God is working in him: "Blessed are you, Simon son of Jonah! For flesh and blood has not revealed this to you, but my Father in heaven" (16:17). Peter is blessed because he is blessed by God. Unlike Jesus, we often underestimate people because we underestimate the working of God in their hearts and minds.

But when Peter denies Jesus, after vehemently denying that he would ever deny him, it seems as if Jesus' trust in him was not justified. Yet Jesus knew that Peter's denials would not have the final word in his life. He was aware of Peter's bitter regret and of the tears following his denial, and after the resurrection Peter is mercifully remembered. The angel of God gives the following instruction to the women at Jesus' grave: "But go, tell his disciples and Peter that he is going ahead of you to Galilee" (Mark 16:7). Peter is mentioned specifically, so that he can be sure that he is still included among the disciples. When Peter and Jesus meet at the sea of Galilee (John 21), Jesus asks him three times about his love for his master, and three times Peter affirms his love—even though he has by now come to realize the imperfection of that love. Three times Jesus entrusts Peter with a special duty in his kingdom. The amount of three confirms that Peter's three denials of Jesus have been cancelled; he has been forgiven completely and reinstated as a disciple. Jesus' faith in his disciple was vindicated subsequently; we read about his courage in the book of Acts, and of his death as a martyr in John 21:19. His days of denial were over.

Yet people also often disappointed Jesus. His was not a naive faith, oblivious of people's sins; he mourned about their unwillingness to be saved. He cried for Jerusalem (Luke 19:41); he lamented the fact that the city he loved so much rejected his message: "How often have I desired to gather your children together as a hen gathers her brood under her wings, and you were not willing!" (Matt 23:37). He knew that the Pharisees and the scribes had to be blamed largely for the sins of the people, and he did not mince his words when he addressed them: "You lock people out of the kingdom of heaven. For you do not go in yourselves, and when others are going in, you stop them" (Matt 23:13). These words should have shocked the spiritual leaders into acknowledgement of their sinfulness, but with their legalistic prescriptions they had built such a strong barrier against knowing God that his words could not enter. In the end, egged on by the chief priests and the elders, the people of Jerusalem preferred a notorious criminal to be released instead of Jesus, and they urged the governor to send Jesus to the cross (Matt 27:17–23). And yet he died for those who rejected him, and prayed for the people by whom he was crucified (Luke 23:34). He believed that there was still hope for them.

One of Jesus' most painful experiences must have been the betrayal by a man from his inner circle, Judas Iscariot. One cannot help wondering about the similarities and the contrasts between the fates of Peter and Judas. Both of them showed regret after their denial and betrayal respectively, but Peter was reinstated, whereas Judas committed suicide. Jesus forgave Peter his denial, but was harsh in his judgment of the traitor: "Woe to that man by whom the Son of Man is betrayed! It would have been better for that one not to have been born" (Mark 14:21). Peter's regret was combined with acceptance of the grace of forgiveness; Judas knew only despair and condemned himself to death.

The Gospels do not reveal Judas' motives for his betrayal clearly. It is quite plausible that he had his own ideas about the calling of Jesus. Maybe he held on to the popular view of his time that the Messiah should chase away the Romans and give Israel back its political freedom. Perhaps he wanted to shock Jesus, by having him arrested, into defending himself, into leading an uprising against the oppressors of Israel. If that is so, he must have felt that all went wrong—Jesus did not defend himself, and he, Judas, had betrayed someone whom he could not help respecting. That could explain why Judas was not reinstated like Peter—not because his sins were too great, but because he kept on holding on to his own demands for the Messiah. He wanted political freedom for the people of Israel and not eternal liberation for all people. Judas was an irretrievable loss for the kingdom.

The Risk of Faith

So Jesus' trust in people was sometimes vindicated, sometimes not. But the point is, if he had no faith in humanity at all, he would not have sacrificed himself on the cross; he would have let the people die in their calamity and sin. The sacrifice of Jesus—or put differently, God's own sacrifice in Jesus—shows that God valued humanity so much that God was willing to take an unbelievable risk—that his unbearable suffering might be scorned, that his invaluable gift might be rejected. God was willing to become vulnerable for the sake of human beings—to offer them eternal life but give them the freedom to refuse it.

Faith necessarily involves a risk; but to not believe is an even greater risk—the risk of missing out on the great gifts of God. The risk of the Christian faith is threefold: faith in God, faith in our fellow human beings, and faith in ourselves. Faith in God is the most fundamental of the three. The person who believes in a God caring for people and working in their hearts has the right foundation to believe in herself and in others—even though that faith may sometimes be disappointed.

Is it worthwhile to believe in and work for a better society? Cycles of evil seem to be never-ending—at the end of a time of oppression we say "Never again"; when similar transgressions are repeated after a while, we tend to say "Alas! Ever again!" But we should beware of relinquishing our belief in transformation—if we become cynical and defeatist, our cynicism will become a self-fulfilling prophecy and nothing will improve, whereas faith in action does bring some light into a dark world. It may be naïve to believe in the coming of a perfect world, but it is realistic to believe in the possibility of a better world; it may be impossible to create an earthly heaven, but it is certainly possible to prevent a hell on earth.

Faith and Prayer

What is the connection between faith and prayer? The Bible says that if we need wisdom we should pray to God, "who gives to all generously and ungrudgingly"—but we should pray in faith, "never doubting" (Jas 1:5–6). Praying in faith seems to set God in motion; God gives when we ask. But why does God demand that we pray? Why doesn't God give without our asking? Doesn't God know our needs?

Indeed, God knows our needs, better than we do, and God does provide much that we do not ask for. We don't ask for a breath of air from moment to moment, yet God gives it to us; but many other gifts are provided in answer to our prayers—because God wants to involve us in God's plan of action, to make us instruments of God's heavenly goodness. Therefore God stimulates us to ask for what we need, and responds in answer to our prayers. Prayer opens the channel between us and God; it ensures continued communion with God.

We are encouraged in the Bible to put our requests to God: "Do not worry about anything, but in everything by prayer and supplication with thanksgiving let your requests be made known to God" (Phil 4:6). So we should earnestly pray to God in order to get what we want. Yet, although we are repeatedly assured in the Bible that God hears our prayers, it does not mean that prayer provides an escape from all suffering. Paul, while he was writing these words, sat in jail for proclaiming the gospel; he knew that suffering for his faith was part of his calling (Phil 2:17).

Jesus told his disciples that God would answer all their prayers, but the promise was given with a qualification: "If you abide in me, and my words abide in you, ask whatever you wish, and it will be done for you" (John 15:7). The qualification is that the disciples abide in him, that they seek his will and that they desire in accordance with his teachings. True prayer is more a matter of being persuaded to God's will than persuading God to do our will; faith in God means that we trust God more than ourselves to know what is good for us. In the ideal prayer of faith, God is moved by our desires and our desires are transformed by God's will; harmony and peace ensue.

Jesus in Gethsemane provides an awe-inspiring example of such a faith. In the night before he was arrested, he prayed: "Abba, Father, for you all things are possible; remove this cup from me; yet, not what I want, but what you want" (Mark 14:36). God did not take the cup away from him, as he wished, and he surrendered to the will of the Father. Jesus' most intense suffering seems to have been in Gethsemane, where his sweat fell like great drops of blood to the ground (Luke 22:44). But once he had surrendered to God's will for him, he seemed to be at peace, and submitted himself freely to those who came to arrest him, accepting that "this is your hour, and the power of darkness" (Luke 22:53). The whole creation was blessed by the unanswered prayer of Jesus, for his suffering led to our redemption. Jesus' days of intense suffering were followed by eternal glory through his willingness to suffer and die for a lost world.

Faith in Hard Times

None of us, however, have the faith, love, and obedience of Jesus. Our suffering can easily destroy our faith; people are, for instance, baffled by large-scale catastrophes like earthquakes and tsunami's, where the good, the bad, and the innocent (children) are struck jointly. Is it a good God that allows such things to happen? Why does God let terrible things happen to good people?

Although we can never find a complete answer to these questions, we should note the great virtue of goodness that can last in times of hardship; the greatest faith is faith that can praise God in the midst of adversity. That is the faith that Paul and Silas showed when they were imprisoned in Philippi: "About midnight Paul and Silas were praying and singing hymns to God, and the prisoners were listening to them" (Acts 16:25). Surrounded by darkness, literally and figuratively, they prayed and praised God—their trust was unaffected by the gloomy circumstances. Such a faith makes an impression; no wonder the prisoners listened to them. And then, while they were glorifying God with the constancy of their faith, the doors of the prison were opened miraculously, and the next morning they were set free. In our worldly way of reasoning, we tend to say: "Let God free me from my horrid situation, then I will praise him." Paul and Silas prayed and praised God first, and then their situation changed; their faith set God moving in a powerful way.

It is important to note that the faith of Paul and Silas had a dramatic effect on their surroundings. The text quoted above mentions that the prisoners were listening to their prayers and hymns; the episode also leads to the conversion of the jailer and his family. Faith in God is not only a matter between God and ourselves; its effect spreads to other people as well. In his letters to various congregations, Paul repeatedly asks the believers to pray for him and his work; he knows that God's blessings are granted in response to the prayers of fellow believers. Through prayer, we take part in God's acts of compassion; if we should stop praying for others, we could be blocking the channels of God's grace. Prayer should therefore be a vital part of our actions for the benefit of the world. God honors us with the responsibility of prayer, but allows us the freedom to neglect it.

Guided by God

True faith in God changes our lives dramatically. It gives a new direction to our lives—we are guided by the Spirit of God. But how does God guide us? In the biblical story of Abraham, the patriarch gets all kinds of instructions from God (like sacrificing his son!); but we as modern people find it difficult to believe in such a direct, unambiguous communication with the Almighty. As a matter of fact, we mostly find people who declare with the greatest confidence that God told them what to do to be misguided. At the beginning of his political career, a rather notorious South African politician of the past told one of his old theology professors that God had told him to go into the politics. The professor listened quietly, and then answered calmly: "Are you sure it was not another kind of noise that you heard?"

How are we to know the will of God when we have to make important decisions? In this matter too, faith begins with the will. Prayer is important, not to give us the right choice in a flash, but to be persuaded by God's Spirit to surrender to God's will. Once we have surrendered, we can think clearly. Faith does not cloud the vision, but clears the mind—for we are often so driven by self-centered desires and anxieties that we cannot think properly. Once we are open to God's guidance, God will lead us to think rationally, help us to consider all the pros and cons in a balanced way, and base our decision on sound moral values. Often the council of wise friends can help us, or circumstances can give us an indication—God may close the way that we wanted to go. And in the end, through the peace in our hearts, God will confirm that the choice was the right one.

Faith in a God of Love

Christian virtues are linked to one another, and they are all linked to the central virtue of love. That also applies to the virtue of faith. From a Christian point of view, one should never talk about "faith" without asking the question: faith in whom? For it is not *our* faith that is so important—what's important is the Person in whom we put our faith. Faith does not concern ourselves only—it brings us into a relationship with God and, through God, into a new relationship with our fellow human beings and with ourselves. Christian faith is faith in a God of love; it is a faith that transforms us into the likeness of God's son, Jesus Christ, who died for our sins out of love; it is a faith that teaches us to love as Jesus did. A false faith has been used in history for all kinds of dubious purposes: to support political agendas and to commit abominable deeds—to torture, kill, and destroy. In those cases, "faith" is used to give credibility to warped desires; but that is not the faith that the New Testament proclaims. The New Testament writes about a faith that leads to love, and a love that leads to faith—faith and love as exemplified by Jesus.

The Difficulty of Faith

The life of faith is both easy and difficult. Easy, because you don't have to earn the favor of God. Easy, because you can cast your worries on Someone who can look after you, and feel secure. Easy, because God will protect you from dangers and comfort you in your suffering. But it is also difficult, because it goes against the grain—at all costs we want to stay in control of our lives. Our natural tendency to egoism and unbelief must be overcome by faith and obedience—and that is difficult.

To illustrate the life of faith, let us use the example of the person learning to swim. At first, when trying to swim, you will panic and sprawl to the side to get your feet on firm ground as soon as possible, where you feel in control of the situation. But gradually you will learn to "trust" the water and experience the wonder of "surrendering" to it. Then you will be carried by the water while swimming in it, and be able to swim where you want to. The water, which you previously regarded as a threat, will enable you to do what you thought impossible—to reach a different shore.

2

Hope

The Centrality of Hope

IN THE *DIVINA COMMEDIA*, when Dante enters hell, he reads the following words on its gates: "All hope abandon, ye who enter here."[4] There is no contact any more between the inhabitants of hell and their Creator, no reason to hope for the improvement of their souls and their circumstances. The most woeful condition is to be lost without any hope. If we despair when we consider the miseries and sins of the world and think that God must be dead, as Nietzsche proclaimed, the darkness is indeed impenetrable. If we are desperate about our sinful condition, only the grace of God can give us hope. For Christians, their God is the ultimate source of all hope.

To Paul, hope is one of the three most important Christian virtues: "And now faith, hope, and love abide, these three," he writes in 1 Corinthians 13:13. We have discussed the virtue of faith, and we know of the centrality of love in Christian ethics; but how does hope fit in? As with faith, it may seem strange to attach so much importance to hope. "To hope for the best" can be quite irrational, because "the best" often does not materialize, as far as we can see—what's the use of hoping then? A while ago I saw a car sticker with the words: "Since I gave up hope, I feel much

---

4. See Dante Alighieri, *Inferno* III.7.

better." For many people, hoping has so often led to disappointment that they do not want to hope anymore—they have been hurt often enough. Better to hope for the worst, they think, so that you can only be pleasantly surprised. And yet the Bible encourages us to hope. But what should we hope for? And what difference does hoping make? Can we change the future by hoping, or does it only make the miserable present more bearable?

Faith and Hope

There is a close connection between faith and hope. Both have to do with believing something that cannot be seen; but there is also a difference. The results of faith are often quite direct; sick people are healed on the spot through their faith, and when Paul says to the jailer of Philippi, "Believe on the Lord Jesus, and you will be saved" (Acts 16:31), the jailer and his household are saved by their faith. The object of hope stretches out to a more distant future: we hope that a difficult situation will ultimately improve; we hope that we won't develop Alzheimer's; we hope for a heaven hereafter. Sometimes the results of faith are not visible on earth, so that faith has to be complemented by hope—Moses, whose faith in God carried him through life, did not enter the Promised Land; and many of God's promises to Abraham, the great champion of faith, were still unfulfilled when he died. Faith and hope also overlap, because hope is not just about the future, it is based on the present, as will be explained. With faith as well as hope, expectation of the future determines the way the present is lived.

A Pie in the Sky

Hope has, understandably, received a bad press over the years. It seems as if expectations of heaven are often projections of unfulfilled wishes. We hate our enemies and want them to burn in hell; our suppressed sexual desires may lead to sexual fantasies about heaven. Should we not rather confront our frustrated desires now and work through them, instead of suppressing them and fantasizing about a future fulfillment?

Furthermore, there is a kind of hope that undervalues this life because it focuses so totally on the life hereafter. People with such a hope believe that life on earth is inevitably full of catastrophes and evil; we have to accept it and find our joy in hoping for a perfect life in heaven. This results in a passive acceptance of the wrongs on earth—there is no motivation to try and improve the world we live in. Such an attitude is often supported by vested interests, for it protects the status quo. The oppressed are kept satisfied, often by the joint efforts of state and church, with the promise of "a pie in the sky when you die," as socialists used to sing cynically. The pie in the sky takes the place of real bread on the table that could still the hunger of the poor.

We should not forget: our earthly life is a precious gift from God, and undervaluing its importance is ultimately an insult to God. And we should also remember that the eternal life in which Christians believe has its basis in the life on earth—*this* is the life that will be transformed in heaven; the good deeds done *here* will receive an eternal glory. The Christian hope is not to be confused with irrational fantasies nor with escapism. So what then is the content of the Christian hope?

Good Lives and Good People

The Christian hope has an emphasis which is different from that of the world; it also deviates from much that is written in the Old Testament, where the hope of the world is often linked to prosperity, to a life free from catastrophe. People generally hope for health and wealth for themselves and their loved ones. These wishes are not restricted to the non-Christian world; they are also very prominent in the Old Testament, where their fulfillment is often viewed as a reward for virtuous people. For instance, in Proverbs 1:32–33 the voice of Wisdom proclaims: "For waywardness kills the simple, and the complacency of fools destroys them; but those who listen to me will be secure and will live at ease, without dread of disaster."

Misfortune will strike those who neglect their duties, the prophet Haggai declares: "My house lies in ruins, while all of you hurry off to your own houses. Therefore the heavens above you have withheld the dew, and the earth has withheld its produce. And I have called for a drought on the land and the hills, on the grain, the new wine, the oil, on what the soil produces, on human beings and animals, and on all their labors" (Hag 1:9–11).

Two points are important in these texts and in many other similar texts in the Old Testament: (1) the desire for good fortune is taken for granted; (2) good fortune is the reward of the virtuous. The wicked may prosper for a while, but at some stage their road will become slippery and they will fall to ruin (Ps 73:18); in contrast, the righteous will prosper "in all that they do" (Ps 1:3).

The Suffering of Job

The book of Job, however, brings a different perspective. Job was "blameless and upright, one who feared God and turned away from evil" (Job 1:1), and he was totally convinced that God, being a righteous God, would notice his virtue and reward him accordingly. For a while that was indeed what happened, but one day, after a deal struck between God and Satan in heaven, one calamity after the other strikes the good man, and he is dumbfounded. Why does God let so many bad things happen to this man who has always served God faithfully? Job is forced to let go of his belief that virtue is rewarded with prosperity. And yet he cannot abandon his faith in the justice of God, and remains hoping that God will ultimately come to his rescue: "For I know that my Redeemer lives, and that at the last he will stand upon the earth; and after my skin has thus been destroyed, then in my flesh I shall see God, whom I shall see on my side" (19:25–27).

Job's hope is still based on his belief in the righteousness of God, even though his experiences seem to indicate the contrary. This powerful statement of Job's hope comes quite close to the view of hope expressed in the New Testament—the hope of Christians that, even though their bodies may perish, they will see God in the end, and God will be "on their side." But whereas the New Testament focuses strongly on the life hereafter, the final perspective of the book of Job is an earthly one. Job gets a material reward—his fortune is restored; he even receives "twice as much as he had before" (Job 42:10). God compensates Job abundantly, in earthly terms, for all the suffering that God allowed in his life.

The Death and Resurrection of Jesus

The life, death, and resurrection of Jesus provide a new perspective to the concept of hope. The most virtuous man on earth was "rewarded" with horrific torture and death; the fate of Jesus destroys the hope that justice prevails on earth. To a certain extent, the Gospels shift the focus of our hope from justice on earth to justice in the life hereafter. Because Jesus was willing to suffer and die for the sake of a lost world, God "exalted him and gave him the name that is above every name" (Phil 2:9). His eternal glory is in proportion to his terrible, undeserved suffering; in heaven he experiences the justice that he was denied on earth. So on the one hand the death of Jesus reveals the extent of the injustice on earth, but on the other hand his resurrection provides us with the hope for eternal justice.

The resurrection and ascension of Jesus is the foundation of the Christian's hope. He who had the strength to conquer Satan, who withstood the demands of the world, who had the inner strength to do what is right and for that reason landed on the cross—he became the ruler of the world. If the history of Jesus had ended with the cross, it would have been devoid of all hope; it would have proved that goodness does not pay, that good people are losers. The history of Jesus would then have been a source of misery, not hope. But the triumphant ending of the story confirms that evil will not have the final say, that goodness will prevail, that we, if we struggle against evil, are battling on the side that will ultimately be victorious; it gives us strength to continue. The testimony of the disciples that Jesus was raised from the dead is a message of hope for good people and of warning for the evil ones, for it declares that the life hereafter is a reality, not a fantasy.

Forsaken by God

Yet it did seem as if Jesus had lost all hope on the cross when he called out: "My God, my God, why hast thou forsaken me?" (Matt 27:46). And indeed, it was a cry of the utmost distress; the darkness enfolding the scene is symbolic of the extreme loneliness and pain in the soul of the Messiah. Yet that is not the whole story. The cry is a quote from the beginning of Psalm 22. Jesus echoes the despair of the psalmist, but the rest of the psalm also reverberates in the anguished call to his Father. Approximately in the middle of Psalm 22 the tone changes from despondency to hope and praise. We may suspect that, coupled with the reproach in Jesus' cry, is an echo of the hope expressed in the psalm: "From the horns of the wild oxen you have rescued me", therefore, "in the midst of the congregation I will praise you" (Ps 22:21, 22). Jesus still knows, even in his darkest hour, that his life is in the hands of his heavenly Father, so that he can die with the words of Psalm 31:5 on his lips: "Father, into your hands I commend my spirit" (Luke 23:46).

The end of Psalm 22 gives yet another angle to the cry of Jesus—we read that the salvation of God's suffering servant will have a worldwide effect: "All the ends of the earth shall remember and turn to the LORD; and all the families of the nations shall worship before him" (Ps 22:27). These words call to mind the global result of Jesus' suffering. His death would lead to a new life for people from "all the families of the nations." We cannot know to what extent Jesus was thinking of the whole psalm while he was suffering on the cross, but we can be certain that the connection which exists between Jesus' cry and the whole of Psalm 22 provides us with a firm foundation for hope. We are reminded that the darkness of the cross was not the final scene in the story of Jesus—it was followed by his resurrection and by blessings flowing to many successive generations.

In the midst of the extreme darkness of the suffering on the cross, a twofold ground for hope emerges: hope for the Savior and hope for humankind. Jesus' obedience unto death is followed by his eternal glory, and his suffering formed the foundation of God's redemption of the world. The first disciples of Jesus experienced a fate similar to his death—they were persecuted, tortured, and killed, but they remained true to their faith, for they were convinced that they would ultimately share in the eternal glory of their resurrected Lord. They also believed that their faithfulness would have a place in God's great plan of salvation. The hope of their Master became their hope too.

Hoping to Be Rich

The hope discussed above is such a spiritual one; is it wrong, then, to hope for material wealth? So many of us can identify with the request to God expressed in the words of the well-known song "If I Were a Rich Man" in the musical *Fiddler on the Roof*:

> Dear God, you made many, many poor people.
> I realize, of course, that it's no shame to be poor.
> But it's no great honor either!
> So, what would have been so terrible if I had a small fortune?
> . . .
> Would it spoil some vast eternal plan
> If I were a wealthy man?[5]

The desire to be rich is not wrong; but when that desire becomes the basic driving force in our lives, it destroys our communion with God. We then don't honor the One from whom all gifts come, but value the gift more than the Giver. For Jesus, the important question is: what, or rather who, takes the first place in our lives? He admonishes his disciples: "Do not store up for yourselves treasures on earth, where moth and rust consume and where thieves break in and steal; but store up for yourselves treasures in heaven, where neither moth nor rust consumes and where thieves do not break in and steal. For where your treasure is, there your heart will be also" (Matt 6:19–21).

Earthly riches have some limitations that heavenly treasures do not have, Jesus reminds us. Earthly riches can be lost—we can insure ourselves against theft, but not against volatile markets and

---

5. Bock and Harnick, "If I Were a Rich Man."

global financial crises. In contrast, no one can rob us from heavenly treasures. While we cannot take our riches with us when we die, heavenly treasures are eternal. Furthermore, when earthly wealth is our prime concern, our idol taking the place of God, it leads to a life of worry and fret, because we are afraid of losing our riches. Desire becomes greed, grabbing takes the place of giving, for the more we get, the more we want—and then we become slaves of our worldly goods. Unlike earthly treasures, which are gained by accumulating, heavenly riches are acquired by giving freely; they bring an eternal joy by sharing and giving; they are free from worry and anxiety.

Jesus assures us that God will care for our bodily needs; we need not worry; we should set our hope on God's providence: "Look at the birds of the air; they neither sow nor reap nor gather into barns, and yet your heavenly Father feeds them. Are you not of more value than they?" (Matt 6:26). God will provide what we need, but God wants us to have a proper sense of values: "Strive first for the kingdom of God and his righteousness, and all these things will be given to you as well" (6:33).

If we look around us, we must acknowledge that many people's hearts are not in the right place. Possessions and wealth have become the gods of modern life. We try to still the hunger deep inside us by buying and accumulating; we adore the magnificent shopping malls, the temples of our time; and instead of dying for our faith, we shop till we drop. In striving to be rich, we have become poor.

Hoping for Good Health

If the Christian hope has such a strong spiritual dimension, what can we hope for in this life? A question that troubles many is: can we hope to be healed of our bodily illnesses? When Jesus was on earth, he cured "every disease and every sickness among the people" (Matt 4:23); can we still hope for that to happen today? The healing power that Jesus displayed on earth did not disappear when he went to heaven; miraculous healing took place through the apostles (Acts 5:12,15), and today he is still the one who can heal the sick. But we should also face the reality that since the time of Jesus faithful followers of Jesus got sick and died; illnesses didn't always disappear in answer to prayer.

Paul, in his first letter to Timothy, refers to Timothy's "frequent ailments," and his advice to the younger disciple may surprise many—he does not advise him to pray harder for his healing, or believe more strongly, but: "No longer drink only water, but take a little wine for your stomach" (1 Tim 5:23). So Paul does not think ailments are a punishment for sins, nor that natural remedies are to be shunned. Illness can become an intolerable burden if we regard it as a punishment from heaven and the lack of healing as a sign of too little faith. People may think that doctors and natural remedies have to be avoided because using them would be a sign of insufficient faith—they think they should trust solely on God to be healed. But the healing power of God is distributed in the curative plants in God's creation, and we should praise God for that as well. The divine healing power is also present in the minds of those who develop medicines and treatments that can cure illnesses.

When we take certain texts out of context, it seems that we can ask anything from God and we will get it if our faith is strong enough: "For truly I tell you, if you have faith the size of a mustard seed, you will say to this mountain, 'Move from here to there,' and it will move; and nothing will be impossible for you" (Matt 17:20). Jesus uses a hyperbole here, as he often did, to bring home a truth powerfully: that miracles happen when we pray in faith. But I have never heard of anyone trying the trick of moving a mountain through prayer; the mountains lifted by prayer are, in the first place, the mountains on our shoulders and in our hearts. Jesus, when the time of his death drew near, asked God that the bitter cup be taken away from him; but he knew that his prayers had to be put in the greater context of God's plan for the world, and he subjected his own wishes to the will of God. Thus it may happen that God allows illness in our lives for a purpose that is hidden to us now but will be revealed one day. We may pray for healing, but we mustn't try to twist God's arm.

Jesus must have been disappointed in people who were merely interested in the healing of the body, who were only keen on seeing miracles; whereas he wanted to repair the broken relationship between them and their God. To the royal official whose son lay ill in Capernaum, he said reproachfully: "Unless you see signs and wonders you will not believe" (John 4:48). Jesus wanted people to believe in God, but they wanted to see signs and wonders. Their interest in health was restricted to the body.

The healing that Jesus wished to give unto others concerned the whole person, not only the body. That is why he said to the ill man whom he healed at the pool of Bethesda: "See, you have been made well! Do not sin anymore, so that nothing worse happens to you" (John 5:14). The illnesses healed by Jesus all point to deeper illnesses of the soul: blindness points to an inability to see the greatness of God, deafness to an inability to hear God's voice, paralysis to an inability and unwillingness to serve God. Jesus does care about the illness of the body—that is why he healed the sick—but he cares even more about the illness of the soul; he is interested in the *whole* person. We should not forget that *heal* and *whole* are related words—Jesus wants to heal the whole person; he wants to heal us by making us whole, by healing us from our inner divisions and making us wholly dedicated to God. When the soul is healed, very often the body is healed as well—the body marred by the tensions and guilt of the soul.

Hoping for Better Times

Can we hope for better times to come, or will such a hope only be fulfilled in the life hereafter? The prophets of the Old Testament and the prophecies of Jesus do not give us much hope for a trouble-free future. The pattern that emerges from the prophecies of the Old Testament is one of painful judgment followed by righteous joy: they pronounce the coming judgment of God on all nations, including Israel, to punish them for their sins; but after the Day of Judgment a remnant of Israel will survive who will serve God faithfully and be blessed with peace and prosperity. After the painful time of exile in

Assyria and Babylon, they will return to Israel, the temple will be rebuilt, and it will be a time to rejoice: "Rejoice and exult with all your heart, O daughter Jerusalem! The LORD has taken away the judgments against you, He has turned away your enemies . . . you shall fear disaster no more" (Zeph 3:15).

The rejoicing did indeed happen, as recalled in Nehemiah 8:17–18; however, in the following centuries, good times and bad times alternated. The temple was desecrated by the Greeks and finally destroyed by the Romans; but the prophet Zechariah provided them with a new source of hope, confirmed by the New Testament. The prophet had a vision of a man with a measuring line in his hand, going to measure the width and length of Jerusalem. An angel stopped the man, intervening with good tidings: "Jerusalem shall be inhabited like villages without walls, because of the multitude of people and animals in it" (Zech 2:4). Jerusalem would have no boundaries; it would be open to all.

This reminds us of the conversation between Jesus and the Samaritan woman at the city of Sychar (John 4:21–24). The woman talks about the debate between Jerusalem and Samaria about the appropriate place to worship God, and Jesus gives her a surprising reply:

> Woman, believe me, the hour is coming when you will worship the Father neither on this mountain nor in Jerusalem. . . . The hour is coming, and is now here, when the true worshippers will worship the Father in spirit and truth, for the Father seeks such as these to worship Him. God is spirit, and those who worship Him must worship in spirit and truth.

At that time, Jerusalem with its temple was the place where God's glorious presence was revealed in a special way; it was the appropriate place to worship God. That is why exile had been such a terrible experience for the Israelites; it seemed to them that they had been far removed from the meeting place between Israel and their God. But Jesus said to the Samaritan woman that a new time was coming when God would be worshipped in spirit. This came about after the ascension of Jesus, when the Holy Spirit was poured out on the disciples and they became God's dwelling place, just as the temple of old was the abode of the LORD of Israel. Therefore Paul can write: "Do you not know that you are God's temple and that God's Spirit dwells in you?" (1 Cor 3:16). From the destruction of the temple a new hope arose.

Yet this new era, the Christian era, has still been full of suffering. The first disciples went through great trials because of their faith. For them it was not difficult to believe that this world is not their ultimate destiny; there was too much injustice, too many tribulations for those who believe. Paul was adamant: "If for this life only we have hoped in Christ, we are of all people most to be pitied" (1 Cor 15:19); and also: "I consider that the sufferings of this present time are not worth comparing with the glory about to be revealed to us" (Rom 8:18).

According to the Bible, we should not lose hope. Though we cannot hope for a trouble-free life on earth, the alternating cycles of good times and bad times will finally end with an everlasting good time for good people.

The World Is Not Our Home

Christians of today who are not persecuted for their faith may find it difficult to echo Paul's words about "the sufferings of this present time." And yet, if we regard this world as our final destination, we are bound to be disappointed repeatedly. There is so much injustice and hardship on earth, and sickness and death remain threatening realities for us and our loved ones. The Afrikaans poet Totius, pseudonym of J. D. du Toit, a professor of theology, was struck by the harshness of death. His one-year-old son died of meningitis, and barely two months later his daughter was killed by lightning. In heart-rending poems Totius questions the ways of Providence and expresses his intense grief. In one of his most famous poems, "Die Wêreld Is Ons Woning Nie," translated as "The Earth Is Not Our Dwelling Place," the poet is filled with sorrow, nostalgia, as well as acceptance. As he notes the passing of the day, the loneliness of a heron, the sadness of a funeral, and the distress of little birds whose nest has been blown to pieces, his observations confirm to him that this world is not our home:

> And I mark this then in every sight
> that rings me round in the failing light,
> the earth is not our dwelling place.[6]

Although most of us are so attached to the world, is there not also a haunting nostalgia deep inside us, echoing the truth that Totius acknowledged: that the world is not our home. We need the hope for a real, eternal home.

Ups and Downs in Psalm 42

The pattern in the history of Israel discussed above—the prophets' vision of alternating darkness and light, of joy and trouble mixed—is echoed by the ups and downs of individual lives. We find a wonderful expression of this experience in Psalm 42. The psalmist is going through a deep depression and feels forsaken by God:

> My tears have been my food day and night, while people
> say to me continually, "Where is your God?" (v. 3)

In such a time, he finds it helpful to think back on previous times when God changed his fortune:

> These things I remember,
> as I pour out my soul:
> how I went with the throng . . .
> with glad shouts and songs of thanksgiving,
> a multitude keeping festival. (v. 4)

Such a memory, such a contrast between past and present, may make many people even more depressed, but the psalmist is sustained by the knowledge of the "steadfast love" of his Lord (v. 8);

---

6. Totius, "Earth Is Not Our Dwelling Place," 24.

he is sure that God will help him again, as in the past. Therefore he rebukes himself for his negative thinking and regains his hope:

> Why are you cast down, O my soul,
> and why are you disquieted within me?
> Hope in God; for I shall again praise him,
> my help and my God. (v. 11)

The ground for the psalmist's hope does not only lie in the past, but also in the present. Even in the darkest of times, when the "waves and billows" of God have gone over him, he maintains contact with God in song and prayer:

> By day God commands his steadfast love,
> And at night his song is with me,
> A prayer to the God of my life. (vv. 7–8)

The Christian hope, like that of the psalmist, is anchored in the present. Hope cannot last if it is not fed by continuing contact with God. Even if we feel that God is far away, as the psalmist did, we are also reminded in the psalm that God is greater and more steadfast than our emotions. The LORD who has repeatedly led us through the "valley of the shadow of death" (Ps 23:4) will lead us safely through darkness again. That also applies to our final hour of darkness—when we die. Then the pattern experienced on earth will be confirmed: a pattern of going through darkness into light—light that flickers unsteadily on earth, but will one day be transformed into eternal brightness.

Hierarchies Turned Upside Down

The first sermon of Jesus recorded in Matthew starts with the Beatitudes, which contain an implicit rejection of the ways of the world (5:3–10). Jesus mentions the people who are blessed in his view, and his list must have gone completely against the grain of the disciples listening to him—it also goes against the grain today. Jesus calls people blessed whom we tend to look down upon; he advocates attitudes that we try to avoid. The first Beatitude states that the "poor in spirit"—people who are conscious of their limitations and their dependence on God—are blessed, whereas we like to be self-sufficient. We want to be happy, but Jesus calls the people blessed who mourn—mourn about their sins and the sins and suffering of the world. The meek are blessed, Jesus says in the next Beatitude, because they will inherit the earth; yet we see how the meek are being trodden down by the powerful, and therefore refuse to be meek. People generally focus on what to eat and drink, and don't like to be hungry and thirsty, but Jesus calls those blessed who hunger and thirst—*after righteousness*! And so the list continues with its revolutionary proclamations, ending with: "Blessed are those who are persecuted for righteousness' sake, for theirs is the kingdom of God." Who on earth desires the blessedness of being persecuted, even if your cause is righteous?

In the Beatitudes Jesus reveals the lopsidedness of the values of this world. The attitudes he calls blessed are not appreciated on earth but are valid in the kingdom of heaven. In God's kingdom earthly histories will one day be reevaluated according to God's eternal criteria—many who are last on earth will then be first, and those who are first will be last, Jesus declared at another time. Herein lies hope for the virtuous, whose values correspond to what Jesus advocated: they will have their reward one day, when earthly hierarchies will be turned right way up.

Remembering the Final Chords

It is emotionally impossible to stay focused on the second coming, hoping that "it may happen today." After some time of hoping has elapsed, hope will inevitably fade away. Hope should rather be linked to the present. In the introduction to one of his novels, titled *Kaas* ("Cheese"), the Dutch author Willem Elsschot wrote that a writer should keep his eyes, from the beginning, on the "final chords" of his story, and that something of the ending should be woven right through the narrative. The same applies to the life of the Christian—the "final chords" of our lives should be born in mind. Our present life should be led in accordance with its ending, when we will be judged by our Creator. The hope for a hereafter is meaningless if we do not conform our present lives to the standards applicable in heaven.

So the most important aspect of the Christian hope is to look forward to meeting God daily—to see God behind our opportunities and challenges, to depend on God's guidance and help, to find God above us, around us and in us. It is a daily hope that stretches out into eternity, for the life in communion with the Spirit of God is the "first installment" of what is to come (2 Cor 1:22).

Two Important Additions

The Stellenbosch Professor of Theology Dirkie Smit gave two illuminating perspectives on the theme of hope which need to be mentioned here. He notes that the Christian hope finds itself between two unacceptable opposites: false hope, and despair.[7] The person with false hope is satisfied with himself and with the world, doesn't observe the need for change and wants to leave things as they are. On the other hand, the person who despairs believes that the world is horrible as well as incurable—nothing will ever change, so rather give up hope.

In contrast, true Christian hope is based on the risen Christ. The hopeful person knows that goodness triumphed in the narrative of Jesus, and that the triumphant Jesus is at work in his followers too—there is no reason for despair. There is also no ground for the satisfaction of false hope, because so much love is needed in the world. The hopeful Christian spreads the love of Jesus—love that relieves the burden of the oppressed and changes lives.

In a newspaper column from 31 October 2009, Prof. Smit discussed a book by the Brazilian educationalist Rubem Alves, *Tomorrow's Child: Imagination, Creativity, and the Rebirth of Culture*.[8] According to Smit, Alves distinguishes between two kinds of hope. People with the worldly kind of hope are impatient; they

---

7. Smit, *Neem, lees!*, 310–12.
8. Smit, "Geestelike waardes."

want to see immediate results, and they sow in order to see the harvest. People with such a hope, Alves says, do not plant date trees, because they take too long to bear fruit; they rather plant pumpkins to have pumpkin pie within a few months. The hope of the Bible, Smit writes, is like the planting of date trees. It is love for the long-term; caring about "one day"; investing in the future of others. If we want the next generation to have dates, he says, we should start planting the trees today.[9]

From a long-term perspective, the immediate future loses its dominant importance. The patriarch Abraham, when he placed his hope on God to provide him with a son, was rewarded for his faith and got his son. When God commanded him to sacrifice his son, he did so, and once more his trust in God was rewarded and he got back his son. But more rewards for his faith and hope would only follow after his death; a nation would be born from the children of his grandson Jacob, a nation to whom God would entrust his word. And with the dawn of the Christian era Abraham, through his faith, became the father not only of the biological Israel, but also of the spiritual Israel who believe as Abraham did (Rom 4). Not knowing what the near or the distant future would bring, Abraham daily led a life of faith and was richly rewarded in the centuries to come.

Bearers of Hope

If justice does not prevail on earth, if the future will never be without its troubles, what should we hope for the world we live in? Should we hope for the end of corruption while we can see how corruption abounds? Should we pray for peace—for example, peace in Israel—when we see no signs of peace emerging? Or must we rather wait patiently for the apocalypse to come and transform the world completely?

We must remember that, while it is naive to hope for a trouble-free, sinless heaven on earth, this world is not totally without hope; it

---

9. Ibid.

is still in God's hands. While we know that people commit evil deeds and that our world is full of uncertainties and catastrophes, we also believe that God is in control, and God is at work in the world—that is the ground for our hope. But it is vital to remember that God wants to work through us; God wants to make *us* the bearers of hope. It is our responsibility to pray for the world, because God acts in response to our prayers. Moreover, we should actively bring the loving presence of God on earth by changing the world around us for the better. Although the struggle between good and evil will continue on earth, in communion with Christ we can be triumphant. If we fail in our duties, hope for the world is indeed lost; then God has, in a sense, disappeared from the earth, as Nietzsche believed. For God is revealed in us and through us, and if the channels between God and us are blocked, God becomes undetectable for the world. Then, once again, God's temple is laid to ruins.

3

Righteousness Etc.

Et Cetera

WE KNOW, OR THINK we know, what "righteousness" means—but what does the "etc." of the chapter title mean? I mentioned in the introduction that the number of seven virtues discussed in the book is to some extent arbitrary, that the virtues are all interconnected, and that one virtue is linked to another. So, talking about righteousness soon turns into speaking about other virtues. Furthermore, different languages do not coincide exactly, like a glove fitting perfectly on a hand. The same Hebrew or Greek word in the Bible, used in different contexts, can be translated differently in various English translations of the Bible; the concept discussed in this chapter is sometimes translated as, *inter alia*, "righteousness" or "justice."

It should be noted that ethical concepts in the Bible are never simplistic; one concept often calls forth its seeming opposite. The prime example here is the biblical connection between justice/righteousness on the one hand and grace/mercy on the other. Righteousness demands that the transgressor gets the punishment he deserves, whereas grace offers forgiveness, undeserved mercy. How these opposites are uniquely linked in the Christian faith will be a central theme of this chapter. The title therefore refers not only to righteousness/justice, but also to grace/mercy. I will use the words "grace" and "mercy," and also "righteousness" and "justice," alternately when discussing the many-sided topic of this chapter.

At the Heart of Ethics

The concept of justice is hard to fathom; yet I would like to highlight some of its central features from a Christian perspective. Justice has a particular relevance to our human condition, permeated by conflicting interests and competing desires. Our desires so easily turn into greed, resulting in an unfair superfluity of power and riches on the one hand, but powerlessness and need on the other. Justice requires the careful weighing up of opposing demands, considering carefully what is right in a specific situation and granting to each what is appropriate. The Romans portrayed Justitia as a blind-folded person with a scale, implying that it is without favoritism; it weighs the opposing demands objectively and balances them with a moral fairness to all. It condemns the oppressor and grants freedom to the oppressed; it denounces the self-centered rich and cares for the helpless poor. It brings balance to an unequal society.

Justice is at the heart of all ethics. Ethical thinking presupposes the ability to put oneself into another's shoes, to have the moral imagination to look at a situation not through your own eyes only, but also through the eyes of another—and that is exactly what the concept of justice implies. The just person strives, in the light of all the relevant information, to let justice prevail—that which is fair to all. The opposite of justice is narcissism, the predisposition to regard every situation in the light of one's own anxieties and desires and to further one's own interests at the expense of others. Narcissism denies the reality experienced and perceived by others, and is therefore, in its denial, closely connected to falsehood; whereas justice is open to the multifaceted truth as experienced by a variety of people. Justice is also linked to humility, because the just person is conscious of the subjectivity of her own perceptions and the limitations of her own knowledge; narcissism, on the other hand, in its tendency to regard one's own perceptions as the absolute truth, is linked to pride.

Justice, Anger, and Revenge

How is the concept of justice related to anger and revenge? Which is right, and which is wrong, and what is the difference? In Romans 12:19 Paul writes: "Beloved, never avenge yourselves, but leave room for the wrath of God; for it is written, 'Vengeance is mine, I will repay, says the Lord.'"

Paul knows the limitations of human knowledge; he realizes that human beings are incapable of pronouncing a totally just verdict on others—God alone knows completely and God alone can judge with absolute righteousness.

And yet, it seems strange that God is allowed vengeance in the Bible, but the children of God are not allowed retaliation. Is there not a contradiction between God's demands and God's behavior? Jesus commands his disciples not to resist an evildoer, to turn the other cheek when they are slapped in the face (Matt 5:39)—should God not also "turn the other cheek" to the sinner, according to God's own commands? One should take into account that the command of Jesus is spoken in a specific historical situation: when Roman soldiers were often violent towards the Jews and made unjust demands on them. Jesus knew that retaliation, in such a situation, would lead to the accumulation of violence, whereas non-resistance could stimulate shame in the oppressor and persuade him to change his behavior.

However, Jesus did not always turn the other cheek. We see that in the Gospel story of the cleansing of the temple—how he overturned the tables of the money changers and drove them out of the temple; the Gospel of John mentions that he made a whip to drive them out (John 2:15). We like to think of "gentle Jesus, meek and mild," but the Gospels tell a different story. The temple was intended to be a place of worship, but the money makers did not use the temple for its intended purpose; with their commercial activities they spoilt the holy atmosphere for those who wanted to praise God. That is why Jesus was so angry with them. They were like the Pharisees, against whom Jesus also vented his anger, who did not enter the kingdom of God and prevented others to enter as well (Matt 23:13).

In his righteousness, Jesus considered the demands of God concerning the temple, the spiritual needs of those coming to worship God, and the greedy behavior of the money changers, and responded accordingly, with anger and controlled violence. His actions were not driven by personal revenge, but by care for God and the godly. It was a righteous anger, triggered by his concern for the honor of God. Furthermore, we must remember that this event came, according to the three Synoptic Gospels, just before the arrest and crucifixion of Jesus. Soon he would sacrifice himself for the sins of the world—and the money makers certainly counted among them. But before he gave his life for the sinners, he vented his anger against them, thus confirming the connection between righteousness and grace, between anger and forgiveness. He had to vent his anger about their sinfulness before he could wholeheartedly forgive them their trespasses.

When Paul mentions anger as one of the "works of the flesh" to be avoided (Gal 5:20), he speaks about a personal anger, driven by personal interests only. But there is a lot of room for righteous anger in the Bible. Not only Jesus had his moments of anger; the wrath of God against sinners is frequently mentioned by the prophets of the Old Testament, and the anger of the righteous against evildoers is often expressed in the Psalms, for instance, in Psalm 137:

> O daughter Babylon, you devastator!
> Happy shall they be who pay you back what you have done to us!
> Happy shall they be who take your little ones and dash them against the rock! (vv. 8–9)

This sounds terribly cruel to a modern ear, but one should note the "extenuating circumstances"—the Babylonians dashed the "little ones" of the Israelites against a rock, and the psalmist wants justice to be restored; what they have done should be done to them.

Hatred is expressed strongly in Psalm 139:19–21:

> O that you would kill the wicked, O God,
> and that the bloodthirsty would depart from me—
> those who speak of you maliciously,
> and lift themselves up against you for evil!
> Do I not hate those who hate you, O LORD?
> And do I not loathe those who rise up against you?
> I hate them with perfect hatred; I count them as my enemies.

One should note that love and hate are intertwined here—the psalmist's love for God is the cause of his hatred towards those who hate God. Looked at it in this way, anger and hatred are not so far removed from loving and caring. If one realizes how repulsive injustice and cruelty are to God and how hurtful to the victim, and one cares about God and humans, the appropriate response is anger, even hatred. The real opposite of the prime Christian virtue of love is not hate, but apathy—not caring about anything. But we have to make the vital distinction between personal revenge, driven only by personal interests, and God's justice, which takes all perspectives into account.

A Reinterpretation of Isaiah's Message

The prophets of the Old Testament proclaimed that justice brings happiness as well as grief—happiness to the virtuous, grief to the wrongdoers. For the people of Israel, justice meant that goodness would prevail and the wicked be punished—the wicked among the Israelites and especially the wicked enemies who caused them so much harm. The Day of the Lord, for the prophets, would be a day when a clear distinction would be made between good and bad people, and everyone would get his or her proper reward. So when Jesus, in a sermon delivered in Nazareth, read from Isaiah 61, the reading would have confirmed the people's expectations of a day of justice to be brought about by a mighty Messiah who would drive away the evil enemy. The chapter in Isaiah is about "the year of the LORD's favor, and the day of the vengeance of our God" (v. 2). The ruined cities would be repaired—"the devastations of many generations" (v. 4). Israel would enjoy prosperity, but the fate of the foreigners would be different: "Strangers shall stand and feed your flocks, foreigners shall till your land and dress your vines; but you will be called priests of the LORD" (vv. 5–6).

In the time of Jesus the people of Israel were oppressed by the Romans, and those who listened to Jesus would certainly have expected the Messiah to free them from the yoke of their oppressors. That was in accordance with the message of the prophets, including Isaiah. Jesus, however, gives a radical reinterpretation of the passage. He focuses on the good news to the poor, the captives, and the blind, and not on the military subjugation of their enemies. On the contrary, he puts the biblical passage into a wider perspective by reminding the congregation of God's mercy to a widow in Sidon and a general from Syria (Luke 4:25–27). Thus he reminds them that there is goodness outside Israel and that God also cares for the "heathens." Moreover, his subsequent death on the cross proclaims a universal human need for salvation, not restricted to Israelites—a need that would remain even when the Romans disappeared from the land. The most fundamental destructive oppressor of the people, Jesus wants to tell them, does not lie outside them, but inside; their sins would still hold them captive even if they should attain political freedom. He was the one anointed by God to provide the forgiveness and salvation which all humans need.

This was a message for which the people were not ready. It was so much easier to blame the enemy than to acknowledge their own sins and their need of redemption. So they got rid of the uncomfortable message by driving Jesus out of their synagogue. Jesus was a healer of the blind, but *their* blindness was one that he could not heal, because they did not want to be healed; their deafness was an unwillingness to hear his message of salvation for all.

The Uniqueness of the Christian Faith

At this moment it is necessary to bring in the Christian concept of *grace*, the seeming opposite of *justice*. Philip Yancey tells the story of a conference on comparative religions where it was debated about what, if anything, was unique to the Christian faith. C. S. Lewis entered the room, and when he heard what the discussion was about, he responded: "Oh, that's easy. It's grace." Yancey then adds the following:

> After some discussion, the conferees had to agree. The notion of God's love coming to us free of charge, no strings attached, seems to go against every instinct of humanity. The Buddhist eight-fold path, the Hindu doctrine of *karma*, the Jewish covenant, and Muslim code of law—each of these offer a way to earn approval. Only Christianity dares to make God's love unconditional.[10]

Does this concept of grace cancel out justice? Does it mean that our conduct does not matter, because we can receive God's favor "free of charge"? We as humans seem to have an intrinsic appreciation of two conflicting concepts—we feel a need to receive grace, but we also have a sense of justice. I would argue that the uniqueness of the Christian faith does not merely lie in the concept of grace, but rather in its unique combination of the seeming opposites of grace and justice.

Jesus Barabbas

The Christian faith is based on an event of prime injustice: the crucifixion of the most righteous man that ever lived. This event reveals the moral inadequacy of all the characters involved in the crucifixion: the spiritual leaders of Israel organizing his death; the bloodthirsty crowd following their false leaders; Pontius Pilate, the representative of Roman justice, too cowardly to acquit the innocent Jesus; and the disciples leaving the beleaguered Jesus in the

---

10. Yansey, *What's So Amazing*, 45.

lurch. Pilate, wanting to free Jesus, gives the crowd the opportunity to choose between Jesus and Barabbas to be set free; and the crowd chooses the latter, a murderer, rather than Jesus the healer.

The crowd's choice between Jesus Christ and "Jesus Barabbas," as he is also called, is mentioned in all four Gospels. Clearly all the evangelists regarded it as an aspect of the crucifixion narrative needing careful attention; here the sinner is linked to the savior. The name "Jesus" means "God is salvation"; therefore "God's salvation" links these two namesakes so completely opposite in nature—the savior and the killer. It suggests that a murderer is included undeservedly in God's salvation. The one Jesus is called "Christ", which means "Messiah," the "Anointed One"—the one appointed by God to save God's lost children. He is the Son of God, created in the image of his Father, called to do God's will on earth. Ironically, Barabbas' name means "son of the father," but this son has lost all contact with his Father in heaven. However, through his contact with Jesus, Barabbas the murderer is acquitted. He is not only freed from prison, but he is freed to live, to make choices, to establish a relationship with his Father in heaven, and start showing the characteristics of the heavenly family. We do not know what happened to Barabbas subsequently. He may have repented, like the murderer on the cross, moved by the suffering of the innocent Jesus and the knowledge of his own guilt (Luke 23:41–42); or he may have continued in his old ways and spoilt his chances.

Barabbas' situation is similar to the crowd attending the trial of Jesus. They are adamant that they want Barabbas to be freed and not Jesus. When Pilate asks them: "Then what should I do with Jesus who is called the Messiah?" they reply: "Let him be crucified!" Pilate, horrified by their bloodthirstiness, washes his hands to show his innocence of the blood of Jesus. The crowd, not impressed by the ritual, responds with a challenge: "His blood be on us and our children!" (Matt 27:15–26).

These are words that make one shudder, but they are filled with ironies and ambivalences unknown to the crowd. Indeed, they are co-responsible for the death of a holy man; with their shouts they have condemned themselves. Like Barabbas, they have blood on their heads. Yet there is another side to the story. Jesus' blood will be on their heads in a way that they do not know and don't deserve. His blood would be spilt to cover them in grace, to remove their sins and guilt. But they, like Barabbas, will have to decide what to do with the mercy shown to them. They have to decide in which way the blood of Jesus will be on their heads—would they be the crucifiers of Jesus or be saved by the blood of the crucified? They too, like Barabbas, are free to live under the grace of God, but it is a freedom that has to be claimed.

Offensive Atonement

Many modern people, Christians included, feel uncomfortable about "being saved by the blood of Jesus"—about Jesus dying in the place of sinners to save them from the judgment of God. They are worried about the image of God created by this doctrine of atonement, of a seemingly cruel heavenly Father who sends his son to the cross. What kind of a father is that? Few earthly fathers, sinful as they may be, would ever send their child willfully to such a terrible fate. But this is a God who condones violence, who includes a cruel cross in his plan of salvation. Why does God not simply forgive sinners when they repent—instead of demanding a horrible punishment? Wouldn't a great God be willing to forgive unconditionally?

There are other problematic elements in the doctrine of the atonement. The doctrine of atonement stresses sin and guilt and conjures up a gloomy picture of human nature. (We will return to this aspect in the chapter on humility.) Furthermore, putting the cross at the heart of Christianity seems to glorify suffering instead of eradicating it. Wendy Farley prefers the vision of the Greek tragedians to a theology of guilt and punishment, and of the acceptance of suffering:

> I am drawn to tragedy because it retains the sharp edge of anger at the unfairness and destructiveness of suffering. I explore a tragic vision in order to find categories for evil that do not justify or explain suffering. Tragedy is not Gnosticism; it is rooted in a deep sense of the value

of creation. Tragedy is driven by a desire for justice, but it does not find this desire satisfied in history.[11]

These are wise words that will be echoed by many. Yet Farley omits mentioning an important aspect of Greek tragedy. The word "tragedy" comes from the Greek *tragos*, which means "goat," and refers to the sacrifice of a goat before the performance of a tragedy. Although "tragedy" indeed "retains the sharp edge of anger at the unfairness and destructiveness of suffering," it also contains suggestions that sacrifice and suffering can be meaningful—the suffering of the tragic hero is a stimulus for the writing of a profound tragedy. The sacrifice of the goat prefigures the suffering of the tragic hero; both are instrumental in cleansing the city and warding off evil. The performance of a tragedy had a cathartic effect, as the philosopher Aristotle explained. There is continuity between the purifying suffering depicted in Greek tragedies and the vicarious suffering and saving sacrifice of Jesus.

Although the doctrine of the atonement has indeed often been formulated in a problematic way, I would argue that we should not discard the doctrine completely; we should rather rethink and reformulate it. We must be wary of throwing the child away with the bathwater. Central in the doctrine of the atonement is the unity of heavenly Father and heavenly Son, expressed repeatedly in the New Testament, especially in John's Gospel. Instead of thinking of God as a Father sending his son to the cross, we should rather think of God as entering the world and sacrificing Godself, revealing to the world the greatness of God's love. By taking on a human form, God has come close to us, participating in our suffering, sharing in our experience of the violence and injustice of the world. The doctrine of the atonement reveals God as more than an almighty Being, far removed from us; it speaks of the incarnate God whom we can praise and worship, even in our suffering. Over the centuries many critical questions have been asked about God's providence. How can we believe in a God of justice in a world where innocent children suffer? Why are evil people allowed to torture and kill? Why do natural disasters cause

---

11. Farley, *Tragic Vision and Divine Compassion*, 13.

havoc and destruction? We cannot find answers to these questions, but are consoled by God's one-word response—the Word who has become flesh.

Justice and Grace

The concepts of justice and grace are complementary. The phrase "unconditional grace" sounds so comforting—it implies an attitude of forgiveness, whatever the transgression. However, if we think it through, in isolation it becomes problematic. Should we forgive someone who willfully does wrong over and over again? Should we forget the harmful effects of wrongdoing and just forgive the perpetrator when he says "I'm sorry"? Somewhere our sense of justice would then feel betrayed. Similarly, it is also unwise to expect unconditional grace from God—it could encourage the evildoer to continue in his ways; he could easily think that evil is not so bad after all. Unconditional grace is cheap grace; Christian grace was attained at an extremely high price.

On the other hand, if we believe in unconditional justice, we also land in deep waters. Only perfect people need no grace—people who never do wrong, never neglect to do what is right, never sin in word, deed, or thought. The ideal of perfection is, obviously, unattainable for us; it would put an unbearable burden on us all. We all need mercy, from God and from one another. Christ's death on Golgotha links grace to justice, and can therefore be a source of great relief. There is a deep joy to be found in the assurance that our accounts have been settled, that we have been removed from the dock.

The crucifixion is the point in the biblical narrative where justice and mercy, righteousness and grace, come together. Although it is a story of the most terrible injustice, of an innocent man condemned to the cross and a murderer acquitted, righteousness in fact does enter the picture. How does this happen? This is a truth unfathomable for the human mind; I can only hope to make a few suggestions that may shed some light on the mystery. If you find it unhelpful, just skip the following pages; there is not one correct, all-embracing interpretation of the crucifixion narrative.

Firstly, we should consider the fact that there is a fundamental imbalance in the relationship of human beings and God. On the scale of justice, the created and the Creator can never have an equal weight; Justitia's scale is tipped precariously. "What do you have that you did not receive?" Paul rightly asks the Corinthians (1 Cor 4:7). There is nothing that we can totally call our own. We received life, we did not create ourselves; from our birth we are debtors. Confronted by the challenges of life, we can struggle hard, but success does not depend on ourselves only. As we have seen in the chapter about faith, the man who completes a marathon and calls out: "I am the greatest!" needed, among a multitude of other things, a fresh breath of air at every step of the way, and even for pronouncing himself great—he could never do it all "on his own"; there are always "outside factors" needed for any achievement. Similarly, it is impossible to attain righteousness before God that we can exclusively call our own.

Furthermore, when we omit to do what we should have done, when we behave unwisely and unrighteous, our balance sheet before God looks all the more depressing. We must remember that Jesus revealed the moral ideals of God for God's human children: to be like Jesus, to behave with his righteousness and compassion, his care for other people, his willingness to bear the pain of the cross for the sake of a world in need. The person who claims to be righteous should be as Jesus was—and who of us can claim that? Who of us are willing to take the road to Gethsemane and Golgotha? Who can be so brave as Jesus was when he confronted the false leaders of his people? So caring for the outcasts? So forgiving toward those who tortured and killed him? If Jesus came to earth only to set an example, his coming was not good news, but bad news. The moral standard for our earthly "exam" was then set higher, and we are all condemned to fail. But now the righteousness of God as revealed in Jesus is linked to God's mercy, and that is good news indeed.

The Christian message of merciful salvation means that God, in righteousness, acknowledges the inequality of the relationship between Creator and creation and takes responsibility for the situation ensuing from the act of creation. Furthermore, it means that God is painfully aware of the fact that the imbalance inherent in the situation has been exacerbated over the centuries by bad choices of human beings, by an infectious evil that has spoilt God's creation, by an accumulation of wrongs. God's solution for the problematic situation lies in the mystery of incarnation: by God's taking a human form, thus adding weight to the human side of the unbalanced scale of Justice. It is the mystery of a sinless God suffering in the place of sinners, footing the bill for their debts and restoring equilibrium to God's creation. Furthermore, we should note that God's justice involves the sharing of our earthly pain, loneliness, and death. Thereby God is revealed as a suffering God, not an almighty Being reigning from afar, living in peace while we are in pain. God's righteousness includes compassion.

But is the unjust crucifixion not at the center of God's plan a justification of injustice? It seems a strange plan indeed—yet the saving sacrifice of Jesus emphasizes the centrality of *relationships* in God's plan with the world; at the heart of the creation lies the truth of the interconnectedness of all beings. We are responsible, not only for ourselves, but also for each other, and the truth of our interconnectedness points to a fundamental moral law: compassion and care for one another. We all know of situations where one person had to help out someone else, when one had to take the place of another who was unable to do what had to be done. The death of Jesus in our place is in harmony with a central law of creation: the fact that we are not "on our own," that we live within a network of relationships—a network that is kept from disintegration by the strength of compassion and grace.

Christianity reverses the natural order of things. In our pride, we want to be virtuous so that God can be impressed by our righteousness—and then pride, the most obstinate of sins, easily becomes the basis or our "virtue." In contrast, the Christian dares to approach God with his unrighteousness, or at best, incomplete righteousness, and accept that the righteous God-man Jesus has opened the door of grace for us. From the acceptance of the vicarious suffering of Jesus follows a life where a fountain of grace continues to flow, where all God's dealings with us are fundamentally motivated by God's grace, where the demands of justice have been incorporated into an overwhelming mercy. The Christian's goodness then flows from gratitude to a merciful God; the continuing grace of God is the source of her grace towards others. Because only those who have received grace can freely give it to others.

The Story of Jonah

God's grace requiring humans to be graceful is a central theme in the beautiful story of Jonah. God commands Jonah to preach to the inhabitants of Nineveh, to warn them of the judgment of God on their sins. Jonah who, as an Israelite, has experienced the violence of Nineveh, refuses to go there, possibly scared by the dangers of the mission. So he rather takes off to Tarshish, but the ship runs into a heavy storm. After a while the members of the crew get desperate; by casting lots they discover that Jonah is the culprit and that his disobedience to God has brought them all in danger. This development confirms our theme of interconnectedness; Jonah's disobedience brings trouble to others. On Jonah's instigation, they throw him into the sea.

So far in the story it seems as if the justice of God determines developments. The people of Nineveh sinned and will be punished; Jonah was disobedient and is thrown into a stormy sea. But then we find a turn in the events. In his seemingly hopeless situation, a fish, commanded by God, swallows him. At first this does not seem to be much of a salvation; but his stay in the fish is symbolic of the "dark night of the soul" where he comes to his senses, realizes his helplessness outside the grace of God, contemplates his sins, and mends his ways. When Jonah reveals a true change of heart in the prayer offered to God in the stomach of the fish, God commands the fish to spew him out on dry land. Jonah is now ready to do what God commanded him at the outset: to go and preach to the sinful Nineveh.

Now we come to the second part of the story. Jonah preaches to the people of Nineveh about the judgment of God on their sins. Through his personal experience he has discovered the power of the Almighty, so that he has no reason to fear the people of Nineveh anymore—what could they do to him, a prophet of the great God? In fact, being an Israelite, he must have enjoyed proclaiming God's judgment on Nineveh—telling them that God would get them back for what they did to the people of Israel. But then two unexpected developments follow: the people of Nineveh repent and the judgment of God is withdrawn. Jonah is horrified, because God has made a fool of him. In contrast to his confession of sins in the stomach of the fish, he now justifies his initial unwillingness to preach to Nineveh. He knew all along, he says, that God could not be trusted to punish the wicked. In his conversation with God he echoes, reproachfully, a phrase repeatedly used in the Old Testament, of God being gracious and merciful, abounding in steadfast love, one that relents from punishing.

Jonah, who has experienced the mercy of God toward him, the disobedient prophet, now finds it hard to be merciful to others; he doesn't understand how God's justice is balanced by God's mercy. Jonah sulks in the beginning of the story, horrified by a command that he thought unfair; he also sulks in the end, when justice is subsumed by grace. The grace of God, shown to him as well as to the inhabitants of Nineveh, has brought him no joy. Jonah wants pure grace for himself, pure justice for others.

Distributors of God's Grace

The Christian's goodness consists of following the example of Jesus—acting lovingly as he did, also taking up his cross as he commanded. Although we can never equal the virtue of Jesus or experience the intensity of his suffering, following him does mean taking a few drops of his cup of suffering. The Christian's suffering can take on a variety of forms. For instance, we suffer when we stand up for what is right in a situation of injustice; we suffer when we share the pain of another; and we suffer each time when we lay down our obstinate wills before the will of God.

Disciples of Jesus share in his pain but also follow him in the distribution of God's grace; they spread a forgiving love that will ultimately conquer the hate of those who persecute us, according to Dietrich Bonhoeffer:

> Through the medium of prayer we go to our enemy, stand by his side, and plead for him to God. Jesus does not promise that when we bless our enemies and do good to them they will not despitefully use and persecute us. They certainly will. But not even that can hurt or overcome us, so long as we pray for them. For if we pray for them, we are taking their distress and poverty, their guilt and perdition upon ourselves, and pleading to God for them. We are doing vicariously for them what they cannot do for themselves. . . . The more we are driven along this road, the more certain is the victory of love over the enemy's hatred. For then it is not the disciple's own love, but the love of Jesus Christ alone, who for the sake of his enemies went to the cross and prayed for them as he hung there.[12]

Compassion inevitably involves pain—caring about the wretched, sharing the pain of the traumatized, fighting against injustice. Is this not unfair, that good people have to suffer? One could argue that the saved don't deserve to suffer—they have been justified, couldn't they "rightly" put in a claim for a carefree life? Yet herein lies a paradox: the followers of Jesus, who are not focused on personal gain, get a reward of the highest value—they start reflecting the nature of the incarnate God and acquire the qualities needed for an eternity of glory. Therefore, by spreading the grace of God they get their just reward. It is not the kind of recompense that the world is looking for; it is the joy of being a blessing to others.

We will pursue this topic of compassionate suffering further in the chapter titled "Joy and Peace."

Forgiveness

Because Christians have been forgiven, the right thing for them to do is to forgive as well, to extend to others the grace which they have received. Jesus goes even further—God's forgiveness towards us depends on our willingness to forgive: "For if you forgive others their

---

12. Bonhoeffer, *Cost of Discipleship*, 166.

trespasses, your heavenly Father will also forgive you; but if you do not forgive others, neither will your Father forgive your trespasses" (Matt 6:14–15). He set the example when he asked his Father to forgive those who crucified him, "for they do not know what they are doing" (Luke 23:34). Jesus knows that the people participating in his crucifixion do not know that he is the Son of God, the Savior of the world, so that there are extenuating circumstances; he distinguishes between the act of killing him and the persons who do the killing. Their act remains terrible, but they are to be forgiven because of their lack of knowledge. Once again the door to grace is opened. Should they find out what they did and repent for their deeds, they will be saved. Jesus wants the grace of God to continue flowing to them in spite of the blood on their hands.

This reminds us that forgiveness should not be determined by the nature of the sin committed. However horrible the deed, Jesus is willing to forgive; according to him, no sin is unforgivable. Forgiveness means not to remain filled with bitterness and revenge, but to develop an attitude of benevolence towards the sinner, hoping for his salvation, granting him a chance to repent. And even if the sinner does not repent, our goodwill should not be restrained by that; for then our lives would be dependent on the reaction of the receiver of forgiveness, and if repentance is not forthcoming our lives will continue to be filled with bitterness. We would be the losers; instead of overcoming evil with good, as the Bible commands (Rom 12:21), we will have been overcome by evil.

If the sinner refuses to repent, that is his problem; his unacknowledged sins will continue to poison his being. But the one who forgives will be liberated by the act of forgiveness. Forgiveness is hard—it is often impossible to "forgive and forget," as the saying goes. Rather, we will forgive and remember and have to forgive again. It may take years, but forgiveness is a worthwhile goal to pursue; it is a lifelong road to inner freedom.

It could happen that the sinner chooses to keep on clinging to his sins, to find his identity in a way of life hateful to God and God's people. Then the distinction between sinner and sin would fall away, for the sinner has identified himself with his sinful ways. The path of grace would then be closed; the sinner would have chosen the hell he receives. In fact, his narcissistic hell would be the best place for him. To him, God's heaven of loving communion would not be heaven, but hell; he would find celestial freedom and joy a drag and a burden. But it is not for us to decide whether a sinner is fit for hell; God only knows. The God of compassion will continue with approaches of grace until the last little flame of hope is extinguished by the sinner's response. The evil person's final home would then be an eternal world of ice, devoid of compassion and care, which Dante portrays in the *Divina Commedia*.

The Issue of Human Rights

What are the connections between *righteousness* and *human rights*, between *justification by faith* and *justice on earth*? These questions will be touched upon in this section and in the following one.

We are living in a world that has become more sensitive to the issue of human rights, where transgressors against basic human rights are prosecuted and brought before an international court. That is an excellent development, that transgressors cannot get away with murder anymore; and yet the idea of human rights, from a Christian point of view, is problematic. On what grounds can we claim to have rights? If it is true, as Paul says, that we have nothing that we did not receive, that our human condition is fundamentally one of grace, can we make any claims at all about our *rights*?

The secular humanistic view of human rights takes humans as its starting point: it focuses on things that we can all "rightly" claim, that every human "must have" if there is to be justice in the world. The Christian view starts not from the bottom, from human beings, but goes from top to bottom. Its foundation is the heavenly grace of God, shown in the gift of life and especially in the salvation by Christ. For those who have received the grace of God, it is right to share the grace of God with others. Those privileged by God's forgiveness should forgive others; those who are loved should give love to the people deprived of it; those who are privileged with material riches should share it with the poor. Having received God's grace, justice demands that we share it with others—that we become distributors of God's goodness on earth.

Justice on Earth

Jesus taught his disciples to pray: "Your kingdom come. Your will be done, on earth as it is in heaven" (Matt 6:10). Looking around us, and turning the pages of history, we realize that the heavenly kingdom of God on earth is more of an ideal than a reality. And yet we should stick to that ideal, strive to realize as much of it as possible, for if we let go of it we will be contributing towards the establishment of hell on earth.

There are times when the light of justice seems to be (almost) completely extinguished in a society. Such a time was the Nazi regime, when behavior that was morally right was declared wrong, and wrong behavior was declared right. In such a time the fundamental distinction between evil and good is replaced by another, ethically neutral distinction: between survivors and those who do not survive. Primo Levi, a survivor of a Nazi camp, describes it well:

> There comes to light the existence of two particularly well differentiated categories of men—the saved and the drowned. Other pairs of opposites (the good and the bad, the wise and the foolish, the cowards and the courageous, the unlucky and the fortunate) are considerably less distinct, they seem less essential, and above all they allow for more numerous and complex intermediary gradations. . . . Here the struggle to survive is without respite, because everyone is desperately and ferociously alone.[13]

It is a time, Levi says, that kills the humanity of the prisoners, because they lose the human potential for compassion and justice. It also kills the humanity of the powerful, because they are coerced

---

13. Levi, *If This Is a Man*, 93–94.

by an evil system to do what is evil. In such a time justice has no power: good people who resist the wrongs are tortured and killed. Bad ones flourish outwardly, but are harmed inside; ultimately, all members of such a society are deeply damaged. It is the duty of all of us to continuously guard against the coming of such a time, such a hell on earth.

There are also other ways in which justice on earth can be thwarted. In a society that is sharply divided between rich and poor, between the "haves" and the "have nots," the sympathy of God for the poor and the helpless is hardly believable for the underprivileged; the love of God for all people becomes dubious to them. It is the duty of the church to restore the belief in a loving God by joining in the alleviation of poverty, supporting the liberation of the oppressed, and resisting everything that limits people's potential to develop to their fullest capacity. The Anglican Archbishop of Cape Town, Thabo Makgoba, put it as follows at his inauguration as Chancellor of the University of the Western Cape:

> Do we sit by while corruption grows, nepotism flourishes, freedom diminishes, and inequality deepens; and be happily, heedlessly, complicit while narrow self-interest, callous selfishness, and the pursuit of personal gain, of power, status, and material wealth, regardless of the consequences for other people or our planet, become the norm? Do we turn a blind eye as cutting corners, dropping standards, sharp practices, become the order of the day?[14]

Two Dangerous Half-Truths

Justice and *grace* are two of the prime virtues of the Christian faith; but isolated from each other, they become dangerous half-truths. Cold-blooded justice towards an individual or a group would lead to a continuing cycle of punishment and resistance, of revenge and retaliation, for without mercy no healing can take place. Cheap,

---

14. Makgoba, "Moral Leadership."

indiscriminate mercy, on the other hand, would strengthen the hand of the wicked and leave the victim vulnerable. The children of God should show neither grace nor justice on its own, but spread God's *graceful justice* on earth.

4

Humility

Reasons to Be Humble

IN HIS BOOK *HUMILITY*, Andrew Murray calls humility the root of every virtue. Yet there seems to be little place or need for humility in our modern society. We have "come of age"; we can look after ourselves. Technology is developing at an astonishing pace; with cell phones and computers we communicate across the globe. We have tamed nature, we are the rulers of the world, and we are venturing into space. No reason to be humble; we can be proud of what we have achieved. And yet, the proud human being is also so vulnerable. Humans are great builders, but high buildings can be destroyed by bombs. They are protected by police, but robbers break into their homes. Although they are able to control technology, they can neither control themselves nor live in harmony with others. Civil wars tear countries apart and terrorism is a worldwide threat. We are the rulers of a world that we are destroying; we have reason to be humble.

False Modesty and Pushovers

The opposite of humility is pride. The proud person focuses on his own glory and dislikes honoring others; he hates to admit his limitations and fancies himself to be better than everyone else. He wants to be honored and hates to be criticized; he overrates himself and underrates others. Yet pride comes before the fall, as the saying goes. The proud person becomes a slave of the community on whose approval he depends; he strives for perfection, and when it proves to be unattainable he despises himself. Humility is the key to balance and inner freedom.

However, over the years humility has been given a bad name, and today it is not generally regarded as an attractive virtue. Associations have been attached to the word whereby it lost the purity of its original biblical meaning as exemplified by Jesus. Humility should be distinguished from false modesty, the pretense that you have no talents at all; humility does not entail a complete submissiveness that allows others to walk over you; humility does not mean that you should despise yourself, neither does it mean that you should love others and hate yourself—the command of Jesus was to love your neighbor as you love yourself. The humility of Jesus had none of the above-mentioned false attachments. He told his disciples: "Take my yoke upon you, and learn from me; for I am gentle and humble in heart, and you will find rest for your souls"(Matt 11:29). It is worthwhile to take a close look at the humility of Jesus and take him as our example.

Jesus told his disciples to turn the other cheek to violent people, so as not to perpetuate and exacerbate violence—he was not in favor of personal revenge. But he was also not a pushover; filled with a righteous anger, he overturned the tables of the money changers and chased them out of the temple, as was mentioned in the previous chapter. Furthermore, Jesus had no false modesty. He wanted his disciples to know who he was, and praised Peter when the disciple declared: "You are the Messiah, the Son of the living God" (Matt 16:16). However, we should remember that the Messiah was the "Anointed One," chosen and sent by God for the deliverance of his people. The glory of the Messiah is not divested from the glory of the One who sent him and who equipped him for the task.

The Father and the Son

Jesus made a statement that would have been regarded as blasphemy by most of the people of his time: "Whoever has seen me has seen the Father" (John 14:9). Jesus has no false humility; he does not deny the fact that he, more than anyone before and after him, reveals the loving heart of God. But once again it should be noted how closely his glory is connected to that of his heavenly Father: "Do you not believe that I am in the Father and the Father is in me? The words that I say to you I do not speak on my own; but the Father who dwells in me does his works" (John 14:10).

The wise words of Jesus and his acts of healing have God as their source. Jesus could not and would not do anything without the guidance of God; his good works had to glorify his God, not himself—as he also taught his disciples: "Let your light shine before others, so that they may see your good works and give glory to your Father in heaven" (Matt 5:16).

The relationship between the Father and the Son revealed a true humility. There was no competition for glory; the Son gave glory to the Father, and the Father to the Son. When Jesus considered the suffering he would face, he agonized, but his main wish remained: "Father, glorify your Name" (John 12:28). And indeed, God's Name was glorified through God's plan of salvation. God's compassion was revealed, for in the suffering of the Son the Father suffered too; and his power was shown, for it was the power of the Father that resurrected the Son. But God also glorified his Son, who bore the brunt of the earthly battle against evil. Paradoxically, Jesus received glory because he was humble, because he did not look for personal glory but desired to do what is right. Through his willingness to be treated as a criminal he received an eternal glory.

Jesus did not put his trust in his own wisdom and strength; in all things he searched for the will of God and prayed for the strength to do it. His close communion with God was clearly revealed in his devotion to prayer. Especially in the Gospel of Luke, the importance that Jesus attached to prayer comes to the fore. Repeatedly Jesus "would withdraw to deserted places and pray"

Humility

(Luke 5:16); before important decisions, like the selection of his disciples, he spent the night in prayer (6:12). In 9:18, 28 and 11:1, we find Jesus praying once again; and in 18:1 he encourages his disciples "to pray always and not to lose heart." Jesus prayed continually to discover the will of God and to receive the strength to do it. His prayer flowed over into his life, where heavenly Parent and earthly Son worked in communion for the healing of a broken world.

In his life of prayer Jesus showed his total dependency on God and his trust in God's guidance. No question of doing his own will, for he knew that even he, the godly man, received what he had from God—his life, his mission, and the strength to fulfill it. On the night in Gethsemane, before he was arrested, he admonished his disciples to "pray that you may not come into the time of trial" (Luke 22:40). He then set an example to them with his prayers offered to God. In his human fear of the excruciating pain lying ahead, he asked God to remove the cup of suffering from him; but he was persuaded in prayer to accept what was necessary for the salvation of humanity, and he received the strength to do what he had to do.

From the example of Jesus we can learn the essence of humility. At the heart of the concept of humility is the realization that we are not self-made people, that we have received what we have, that we can call nothing truly our own. The humble person recognizes God as the giver and sustainer of life and lives in conscious dependence on and harmony with God. The opposite of humility is pride: the tendency to elevate ourselves, the desire to appropriate for ourselves the life that we have received; ultimately, the yearning to place ourselves on the level of God, and God on our level—or rather on a level below us, where we can control God. The humble person, in contrast, realizes how small he is, just a spot in the vast universe, and how great the God is who created the universe. She is filled with amazement because the Almighty notices her and cares for her needs and has granted her a place in the eternal plan of salvation; whereas wonder and awe have no place in the heart of the proud one.

Vulnerable Creatures

I have known a man who had an important position and was used to giving orders. Then he got seriously ill; and as he was lying in hospital, his knee started itching. In his words: "Then I told my finger to scratch my knee; but the finger replied: 'Do your own dirty work.' And I could not, for the life of me, get to the place where it itched."

This illness brought about a complete change in his life. He realized what a vulnerable creature he was, not at all as high and mighty as he had thought. He experienced how an illness could incapacitate him, and in his helplessness he took the risk—to shift the object of his trust from himself to God. He started relying on God, not only for big issues, but also for the little things in life. Over the following years the realization of his own vulnerability was confirmed and his trust in the greatness of God vindicated.

Good News for the Humble

The good news of the Bible is only good news for the humble, as we see in God's invitation to humanity in Isaiah 55:1: "Ho, everyone who thirsts, come to the waters; and you that have no money, come, buy and eat! Come, buy wine and milk without money and without price."

In verse 2 the reader is promised water that will quench her thirst—and added to the water necessary for survival is the promise of abundance: wine and milk and food that will continue to satisfy. Astonishingly, the invitation goes out to those without money; hunger and thirst are the prerequisites for getting this priceless meal. The spiritual food referred to is not meant for the complacent and the self-satisfied—for only empty hands will be filled.

If one links this promise to the Gospel narrative of the crucifixion of Jesus, an extra meaning is added to it. The abundance promised here did in fact have a huge cost to it: the death of the Son of God. From the richness of his virtue he paid for those who were bankrupt. When he died, the curtain of the temple was torn in two (Luke 24:45)—the holiest part of the temple, where only the high priest was allowed to enter (and only once a year), was now opened for all by the sacrifice of Jesus; everyone could enter into the presence of God and receive an eternal life of communion with the Creator. That is the full meaning of the food and drink that Isaiah referred to, which will satisfy the deepest hunger and which is free—what has been paid for will never have to be bought again.

The invitation to humbly accept the gift of God instead of trying to earn it does not mean that we are totally passive recipients of the grace of God. We are more than puppets: God calls us, and waits on our response; with astonishing humility, God is dependent on us. It is a mutual relationship of giving and receiving in which humility and glory are intertwined. The glorious God is humble, and humble humans are glorified.

Somber Good News

The Christian message is about undeserving sinners and the perfect Son of God. The good news, however, contains a danger: it can lead to a totally negative view of humanity, a somber look at ourselves and the world. Philip Yancey retells a story heard by a friend:

> A prostitute came to me in wretched straits, homeless, sick, unable to buy food for her two-year-old daughter. Through sobs and tears, she told me she had been renting out her daughter—two years old!—to men interested in kinky sex. She made more renting out her daughter for an hour than she could earn on her own in a night. She had to do it, she said, to support her own drug habit. I could hardly bear hearing her sordid story. For one thing, it made me legally liable—I'm required to report cases of child abuse. I had no idea what to say to this woman.
>
> At last I asked if she had ever thought of going to a church for help. I will never forget the look of pure, naive shock that crossed her face. "Church!" she cried. "Why

would I ever go there? I was already feeling terrible about myself. They'd just make me feel worse."[15]

For this woman, the church's condemnation of sin completely obliterated the other side of the gospel story, namely God's grace to sinners. She is not alone in her view. For many, the message of the church is a somber one, a story of human failing and sin, of condemnation and hell for the sinner, and of a world that is lost. Their interpretation of Christianity does not come as a complete surprise. Paul, for instance, in his eagerness to persuade people not to build their trust on their own virtue, paints a bleak picture of human nature. Quoting bits from the Old Testament, he writes in Romans 3:10–13:

> There is no one who is righteous, not even one;
> there is no one who has understanding, there is no one who seeks God.
> All have turned aside, together they have become worthless;
> there is no one who shows kindness, there is not even one.
> Their throats are opened graves; they use their tongues to deceive.

This view was echoed by many eminent theologians. Calvin's famous *Institutes of Religion* commences with the following statement: "Nearly all the wisdom—that is to say, true and sound wisdom—that we possess consists of two parts: the knowledge of God and of ourselves."[16] It is in the light of the wisdom, purity, and righteousness of God, Calvin maintain, that we discover our own vanity, ignorance, and depravity.

Blaise Pascal had a similar view and said: "To know God without knowing the wretchedness of humankind breeds pride. To know the wretchedness of humankind without knowing God breeds despair. To know Jesus Christ constitutes the middle course, because in him we find both God and our wretchedness."[17]

---

15. Yancey, *What's So Amazing*, 11.
16. Calvin, *Institutes*, I.1.i.
17. Pascal, *Pensées*, no. 526.

Jesus and Sinners

Such a negative view of human nature could be very depressing; no wonder the prostitute mentioned above was scared to enter a church. When humility leads to contempt for oneself and for others, it loses all its value. Furthermore, to believe that the world outside Christianity is basically depraved and lost could make it quite difficult for Christians to live and interact in a world that has become increasingly secular. It may be a consolation for many to know that Jesus did not have a totally negative view of human nature.

We should note that sinners felt at home with him. He called Matthew the tax collector to be his disciple, although tax collectors were hated because they generally enriched themselves with excessive taxation. As a token of friendship, Jesus had a meal with Matthew, and they were joined by "many tax collectors and sinners" (Matt 9:10). When the Pharisees reproached Jesus for eating with sinners, he replied that he was sent to heal sinners, not to call the righteous. The tax collectors as well as the Pharisees were sinners; the fundamental difference was that the tax collectors knew it, but the Pharisees, who meticulously obeyed the rules of the law, did not—unaware of their hypocrisy and mercilessness, they regarded themselves as being righteous, and could therefore not be healed.

Of course, the mercy of Jesus towards tax collectors and sinners did not mean that he condoned the sins that they committed. When Jesus spent the day with Zacchaeus the tax collector, it led the sinner to acknowledgement of guilt and to restitution: "Look, half of my possessions, Lord, I will give to the poor; and if I have defrauded anyone of anything, I will pay back four times as much" (Luke 19:8). And when Jesus showed mercy to an adulterous woman, he admonished her: "Do not sin again" (John 8:11).

In an early sermon to the people of Nazareth, Jesus pointed out that God had sent Elijah, in a time of severe drought, not to anyone in Israel, but to a "heathen," a widow in Sidon; and that Elisha did not cure a leper in Israel, but only one from Syria (Luke 4:25–27). Jesus wanted to warn them against self-righteousness and to remind them that God also appreciated people outside the covenant of Israel. When he experienced the humble faith of the Centurion in Capernaum, Jesus declared: "I tell you, not even in Israel have I discovered such a faith" (Luke 7:9). Clearly, not everyone outside the faith of Israel was wicked. Jesus also did not believe in the total depravity of all people who had not (yet) experienced the salvation through him. When he met Nathanael, he commented on the future disciple's integrity: "Here is truly an Israelite in whom there is no deceit!" (John 1:47). Jesus did indeed declare that "no one is good but God alone" (Mark 10:18), but the fact that no one is (completely) good does not mean that everyone is completely bad.

The Greatness of John the Baptist

Jesus' comments on John the Baptist, who lived before the salvation of Jesus through the cross and his resurrection, are quite revealing in this respect. Jesus does not regard John as a depraved and lost sinner; on the contrary: "Truly I tell you, among those born of women no one has arisen greater than John the Baptist; yet the least in the kingdom of Heaven is greater than he" (Matt 11:11). Jesus recognizes the greatness of John—he is the greatest of the prophets, the one who prepared the way for the Messiah. Like Jesus, the Baptist would later pay with his life for his righteousness: he was put in jail when he bravely criticized the transgression of Herod, who had unlawfully taken the wife of his brother, and was executed because the ruler's wife hated him for his criticism (Matt 14:3–4, 8). Indeed, he was a good man.

And yet, "the least in the kingdom of God is greater than he." What could that mean? It is significant that Jesus links John the Baptist to "those born of women." The core of salvation is for Jesus the concept of rebirth—a birth not by women, but by the Spirit of God, where greatness is given to those willing to be "the least." Jesus explained this mystery to Nicodemus (John 3:3–6):

> "Very truly I tell you, no one can see the kingdom of God without being born from above." Nicodemus said to him, "How can anyone be born after having grown old? Can one enter a second time into the mother's womb and be

born?" Jesus answered, "Very truly, I tell you, no one can enter the kingdom of God without being born of water and Spirit. What is born of the flesh is flesh, and what is born of the Spirit is spirit."

By being born of the Spirit, people of the kingdom receive an unheard-of greatness. They are "the least in the kingdom of Heaven," but will truly be the greatest.

Birth and Death

This birth of the Spirit is intertwined with death—the death of our natural instinct to be "the greatest" and to be in control of our lives. It involves us humbly surrendering all that we have and are to the reign of God, so that the Spirit of God can enter our lives; for we cannot be guided by God's Spirit while sticking to the control of our lives. The central paradox of the gospel of Jesus is the fact that when we lose our lives we will have them, as Jesus said according to Matthew 16:25.

Jesus explained the intimate connection between birth and death with the metaphor of a grain of wheat: "Very truly, I tell you, unless a grain of wheat falls into the earth and dies, it remains just a single grain; but if it dies, it bears much fruit" (John 12:24). Jesus was talking about his own death, which would prove to bear fruit in abundance; but his words are also applicable to the spiritual death and rebirth needed in the lives of his followers. Symbolically, a proud grain of wheat would try to become a bigger and better grain of wheat. But Jesus says, before it can start sprouting, before it can grow up towards the sun, it has to fall into the ground to be transformed into a completely different mode of being. Then only can it bear fruit—be a blessing to others instead of remaining imprisoned in a self-centered life. Falling into the earth is an image of humility—of moving into the "dark night of the soul," where one has to realize that one cannot save oneself, where one has to let go of personal wishes and demands, before the miracle can happen; when the grain is not merely being preserved, but transformed fundamentally. This metamorphosis does not entail a loss of identity, but an attainment of the identity that God from all eternity had in mind for the person—the realization of all her hidden potential.

In this death and rebirth we follow in the footsteps of Jesus, as Paul explains in his letters to the Romans: "For if we have been united with him in a death like his, we will certainly be united with him in a resurrection like his. We know that our old self was crucified with him so that the body of sin might be destroyed, and we might no longer be enslaved to sin" (6:5–6).

This death of the "old self" goes against the grain of human nature. Survival is a fundamental instinct, and to survive we look after our own interests and control our own lives. The seemingly illogical message of attaining life through losing life is therefore completely unacceptable to the old self, "the flesh." As Paul says, "the mind that is set on the flesh is hostile to God; it does not submit to God's law—indeed it cannot" (Rom 8:7). We should note that "the flesh" here does not refer to the body (Paul has nothing against our wonderful, God-given bodies); it is a synonym for the old self. When Paul focuses on the contrasting desires of the flesh and the Spirit, the distinction is therefore not between body and spirit, but between the desires of the "natural human," who wants to be "captain of his soul," and the desire of the Spirit of God, who wants to raise us to a higher level of existence. Human nature by itself cannot attain the life of the Spirit, the life through death of the old self—we have to be led and helped and elevated by the Spirit of Christ. Indeed, both sides of the message of the gospel—forgiveness of guilt and liberation from sin—are meant for the humble, for those who realize that they cannot help themselves. C. S. Lewis explains it quite clearly: ". . . what do we mean when we talk of God helping us? We mean God putting into us a bit of Himself, so to speak. He lends us a little of his reasoning powers and that is how we think; He puts a little of his love into us and that is how we love one another."[18]

But God's love and God's reasoning in God's eternal existence, would be totally strange, unknowable to us, earthly beings;

---

18. Lewis, *Mere Christianity*, 56.

God has to be incarnated, God's love has to become flesh, for it to have meaning for us. Lewis writes: "Supposing God became a man—suppose our human nature which can suffer and die was amalgamated with God's nature in one person—then that person could help us. He could surrender his will, and suffer and die, because he was man; and he could do it perfectly because He was God."[19]

What we cannot do by nature, the man-God Jesus could; and when the Spirit of Jesus enters our beings, the result is dramatic. In the formulation of Lewis, we will not become nicer people, but new humans:

> For mere improvement is not redemption, though redemption always improves people even here and now and will, in the end, improve them to a degree we cannot yet imagine. God became man to turn creatures into sons: not simply to produce better men of the old kind but to produce a new kind of man. It is not like teaching a horse to jump better and better but like turning a horse into a winged creature. Of course, since it has got its wings, it will soar over fences which could never have been jumped and thus beat the natural horse at its own game. But there may be a period, while the wings are just beginning to grow, when it cannot do so: and at that stage the lumps on the shoulders—no one could tell by looking at them that they are going to be wings—may even give it an awkward appearance.[20]

We must, however, guard against some misconceptions about being born again. It does not necessarily entail a dramatic incident; and it is not a single, once-in-a-lifetime event. God works in so many ways with humans that we cannot compress God's salvation into one form only, for instance, the dramatic kind of conversion that Paul experienced on the road to Damascus. Furthermore, rebirth is a lifelong process: just as our bodily cells continually die and are replaced by new cells, so the spiritual life is sustained

---

19. Ibid., 57.
20. Ibid., 180–81.

through a daily experience of life through death, of surrendering our will to God so that God's life can fill us. And we do not become perfect on earth—just as well, for being perfect would provide a strong temptation to pride, to elevating ourselves above the other imperfect human beings. Rather, we have to come to God daily, in our brokenness and our need, to be helped. Because we are wounded, we can sympathize with a wounded world; because we struggle, we can reach out compassionately to others who struggle. And slowly, gradually, we change into the loving person that the eternal God wishes us to be.

It becomes clearer now why many theologians have despised human nature—not because humans are intrinsically bad, but because they are naturally averse to a life where control is surrendered to God. The novelist Marilynne Robinson, in an essay in which she hopes to revive interest in John Calvin, explains:

> Theology of the period of Cauvin (Calvin) employs a characteristic language which discredits it in the eyes of modern readers.... The first thing that must be born in mind is that those who wrote in such terms, whether Cauvin or Luther or John of the Cross, did it in the service of an extraordinarily exalted vision of the human soul.... The disparagement of "the flesh" is one half, an intrinsic part, of an assertion about human nature which exalts it above all perceivable reality.[21]

The need for the old self to die does not mean that we have to despise human nature; as was mentioned previously, humility does not entail contempt for oneself or for others. It is said that St. Francis of Assisi, filled with sympathy for his body, which had to go through so many hardships, used to call it "*brother* donkey." Similarly, we could talk about "brother/sister old self." The poor old self cannot possibly accept the thought of dying, because it goes against its basic survival instinct—so we will find that a part of us desires a spiritual life and another part of us dreads it. Therefore, we must lead brother old self compassionately to God who is calling him, to the only One who can save him from himself. Sister

---

21. Robinson, "Marguerite de Navarre," 182, 184.

old self will at first be like a pet recoiling from the vet, fearing the one who wants to help; but gradually, as she discovers that the vet is not an enemy, but a friend, she will more and more willingly take the injections needed to be healed.

The Transformation of Individualists

Rebirth transforms our individualism, our tendency to do our own thing and go our own way. Individualism is not a totally negative quality, since it helps us to take responsibility for our lives, but it can easily be tempted by selfishness and pride. Individualists tend to regard themselves as the center of the universe; they care primarily for their own interests—other people should look after themselves. In contrast, the humble person realizes her *interconnectedness*—that she is a speck in a vast universe created by the God to whom she belongs; that she is linked to the rest of humanity sharing the world with her, and that she is also connected to past and future generations. She knows that there is no clear divide between individual and societal well-being; the one facilitates the other. She does not make a distinction between caring for herself and caring for others, because she sees all people as part of the creation of God, and she cares for them all.

The proud person sees himself as the measure of all things, and despises those who are different; the humble person knows his own limitations and rejoices in the diversity of creatures, seeing the image of God in everyone, even though the image may be distorted by sin. The proud person sees nature—the animals, the plants, the soil and the water—only as objects to be utilized; the humble person sees in nature a revelation of the glory of the Creator and tries to preserve its beauty.

Intellectual Pride

Pride easily takes hold of the intellect; in our pride we tend to think that we know and understand everything. The humble person realizes the limitation of his own knowledge and is keen to learn from others; but also knows that even the accumulated knowledge of humanity can only cover a tiny fragment of reality. Humble researchers admit that as they cover new ground and make new discoveries, they also discover more and more how much they do not know. The little spot lit by our knowledge and insight is surrounded by an enormous world of darkness.

When Job is struck by disaster, he struggles to understand the biggest of mysteries: If God is almighty and good, why does God allow so much suffering? Why are bad people often prosperous and why do good people suffer undeservedly? Job struggles, argues, and racks his brain—and then God enters the scene with a paradoxical response. Job receives praise for the way he has spoken about God (Job 42:7); clearly, God likes Job's questioning mind. But God also puts Job in his place and rebukes him for putting himself on the level of the Creator: "Where were you when I laid the foundation of the earth?" (38:4). In comparison with God, Job knows nothing; as a matter of fact, he is arguing with the reasoning powers granted to him by his Creator.

Thomas of Aquinas, having almost finished his great theological work, the *Summa Theologica*, had a heavenly vision while he was having Mass. We don't know what he saw, but it must have been a profound vision of the glory of God's plan for the world. After that, Thomas stopped writing altogether, for "all that I have written seems like straw to me," he told his secretary. For us, his straw is of the best possible quality, but we must not forget that it can never contain the grandeur and mystery of God's creation and that no mind can penetrate God's unfathomable works.

The search for knowledge and understanding is basic to the enquiring human mind. It is not wrong to want to know more, but wrong to overestimate what we know. We hope for a "theory of everything," whereas there is not a single thing that we understand completely—least of all ourselves. We may be able to discover causal links between occurrences and predict future events, but we do not know the ultimate cause of the causal links, and we are often baffled by unpredictability. If we convince ourselves of our supreme insight and knowledge, we fool ourselves and lose the sense of wonder and awe that the universe stimulates in humble people.

There are scientists who think their theories contain no loopholes and who are scathing in their response to those who dare to criticize them. There are politicians who invent far-reaching ideologies with the pretense of a simple solution to all problems. However, such ambitious, sweeping ideologies have caused much suffering, for they exclude concrete facts and individual needs. An example from the South African past is the ideology of "Grand Apartheid."

The intellectual search for knowledge and understanding often takes a route similar to the spiritual road of the Christian. The light of new understanding is followed by the darkness of a new lack of understanding, which may lead to new understanding, and so forth. The intellectual life, like the spiritual life, is characterized by a continual death and resurrection. We never reach the point of ultimate knowledge; to reach a final point would mean the end of all intellectual endeavors. Every scientist, philosopher, and theologian only plays a humble part in an ever-unfolding world of knowledge.

Washing Feet

In John 13, in a vivid biblical scene, Jesus shows his disciples the content and the cost of humility—he washes their feet during their last Passover meal together, just before he is crucified. The event is clearly linked to the crucifixion. In the previous chapter we read that Jesus is anxious about his coming suffering and death (12:27); he is contemplating his reasons for obeying the terrible command of God. He knows that his message is characterized by service (12:26) and realizes that the only way to bear fruit is through death (12:24). Now he has to convey this message to his disciples, who are still so keen to be served, who want to be the most important people in the world, as we see in Luke 22:24.

When Jesus takes off his outer robe, ties a towel around himself, and starts washing and drying the feet of the disciples, he takes on the role of a slave. Jesus thereby relinquishes all his rights—for a slave has no rights; he is the possession of the master whom he has to serve. A slave has no choice; however, for Jesus it is a deliberate choice; he is a "free slave," willing to be humiliated for the salvation of the world. He knows that sticking to his rights would mean refusing the saving injustice of the cross. The scene reminds us of the famous description of Jesus by Paul in Philippians 2:6–8:

> ... who, though he was in the form of God,
> did not regard equality with God
> as something to be exploited,
> but emptied himself,
> taking the form of a slave,
> being born of human likeness.
> And being found in human form,
> he humbled himself
> and became obedient to the point of death—
> even death on a cross.

The motivation for Jesus' willingness to humble himself unto death was love—he loved without limits, "to the end" (John 13:1). When Jesus washes his disciples' feet, he wants to carry over his attitude of limitless love to them; it is a purifying act, one that gives the disciples a share with their master (13:8). It is a ritual that will stick in the memory of the disciples, which they will understand later (13:7) when they will go into the world to serve, when they will also suffer for the gospel, like Jesus; when they will also be like grains of wheat that die before they bear fruit (12:24). Jesus humbles himself so that they will be humble, so that they will be cleansed of their pride.

Jesus died not only for his disciples, but also for all who would believe afterwards; in a sense, all Christians' feet have been washed by Jesus, because he humiliated himself for all of us. So the admonishment of Jesus also applies to us: "If I, your Lord and Teacher, have washed your feet, you also ought to wash one another's feet" (13:14). If he who was called "Son of God" was willing to act like a slave and die like a criminal to save us, we should be humble as well; we owe it to him to start washing the feet of others.

In this way we will spread the cleansing act of Jesus, because true humility can be infectious—instead of fighting for our own rights, prompting others to fight back, we relinquish and sacrifice and inspire others to do the same.

We should be driven by the desire to serve; we should humble ourselves in love. Such humility goes completely against popular demands. Most people strive to have power and status; they stand upon their rights. The example of Jesus to his followers is different: his love is without limits; he goes "to the end" to provide in the needs of a desperate world. It is a glorious love because it does not look for its own glory.

Our Time in God's Hands

In conclusion, we should look at the time management of Jesus, who invited us to take his yoke upon us and learn from his humility. In this respect too, his life is characterized by humble dependence on God. Jesus discovered the will of God during many hours of prayer, and these prayers generated a continual life of communion with God, where he did God's will and, from moment to moment, received from Above the strength, wisdom, and love that he needed for his task. His time was in God's hands.

This is the example we should strive to follow. We tend to think: "My time is my own." On the contrary, the time that we have is a gift from God, and when we hand back to God what God gave to us first, when we surrender our time to God, the miracle happens. Instead of worrying about the past or the future, we focus, minute by minute, on serving God in all that we do. We pause regularly during the day to be reminded whose time we are spending. We wait on God to guide us in what to do and what to leave; that should be part of our business of serving God. Instead of rushing to get everything done, we trust God to help us to complete what has to be completed. Time, which we cannot hold on to, which passes so inexorably, is then filled with the splendor of eternity, of that which does not pass. Our earthly time becomes eternity incarnate, an earthly revelation of the eternal will of God.

5

Joy and Peace

Sorrow and Joy

In Galatians 5:22, when Paul writes about the fruit of the Spirit, the three that he mentions first are love, joy, and peace. The virtue of love permeates all the chapters of this book, but joy and peace are the specific themes of this chapter. Like most of the Christian virtues, they are not simplistic concepts; they are intertwined with sadness and sorrow. In his letter to the Philippians, Paul stresses the importance of joy: "Rejoice in the Lord always," he says (Phil 4:4); and he sets the example: "I rejoice in the Lord greatly" (4:10). However, as he was writing this letter, he also had reason to be sad, for he was kept in prison. As an apostle, he had to experience many "afflictions, hardships, calamities"; he was "sorrowful, yet always joyful" as we read in 2 Corinthians 6:4, 10.

I know a woman who, when I ask her how she is, usually replies: "I'm always on top of the world—praise the Lord!" I have never had the courage to ask her if she thought herself better than Jesus, who was not always on top of the world, who sweat blood in Gethsemane and felt far from God on Golgotha. In contrast, there is an Afrikaans short story by Johannes van Melle titled "Oom Diederik leer om te huil" ("Uncle Diederik Learns to Cry"). The story is set in 1918, during the Spanish flu, which killed many people in South Africa. With so many people dying around him, Diederik has a dream with a clear relevance to his situation. He dreams that he was going "where all people go": a large church on top of a hill—clearly symbolic of death and the life hereafter. He travels through many a gate, and at every gate he has to answer questions about his life and the fulfillment of his duties. The questions at the first few gates are all about his loyalty to the cause of the Afrikaner people, and Diederik answers these questions confidently. But gradually the circle is widened—later he is questioned about his attitude towards his black workers, and he barely passes through that gate. At the last gate he cannot answer the question: "Why don't you cry?" The man at the gate informs him: "We only let people through who cry," and tells Diederik to go home to learn to weep.

When he wakes up, Diederik is confused about the meaning of the dream and consults his pastor. When the pastor reads a verse from Luke 19 the meaning of the dream dawns upon him: "When Jesus came near and saw the city, he wept over it." Diederik realizes that a Christian should weep for a world worn down by suffering and sin, and a great sadness comes over him because he has never learned to cry. This sadness about his lack of compassion is a first step towards fulfilling the demand of the man at the gate—to be moved to tears by the sorrows of the world.

Paul says joy is a fruit of the Spirit; Van Melle says sadness flows from compassion—who is right? Is joy good and sadness bad, or is it maybe the other way round? What is the nature of the Christian's joy? These are the central questions of this chapter. At the outset we should consider that Jesus spoke about his complete joy (John 15:11) but was also known as a man of sorrows (Isa 53:3). Perhaps the Christian ideal is not a sorrowless joy or a joyless sorrow, but a combination of joy and sorrow.

In the chapter about "Hope" we saw that the Christian's hope differs from that of the world—the latter is focused on worldly things, on health and wealth; the Christian's hope has a different perspective. A similar difference appears when comparing the joy of the world and the joy of the Spirit: the joy of the world is determined by outward circumstances; the Christian virtue of joy is not solely determined by fortune and misfortune, so it has a greater stability. However, as in the chapter on "Hope," we must emphasize: it is not wrong to be happy when things go well or be disappointed when calamity strikes, but these natural emotional reactions contain no virtue; the Christian virtue of joy transcends them.

Worries that Keep Us Going

Let us consider attitudes and thought patterns that kill all joy and have to be guarded against. Perhaps the greatest killer of joy is worry. Some people worry about everything; worry is to them like a rocking horse—it keeps them going though it brings them nowhere. Others worry about specific areas of their lives; the things that are the most important to them naturally cause the most anxiety. Some people worry only about themselves; others worry about their dear ones as well; some people carry the load of the whole world on their shoulders.

Worry is not something to be ashamed of; having no worries at all may rather be a cause for concern, since that could indicate indifference. An amount of anxiety is natural, even desirable—it shows that we care. Worry is not unconnected to joy, for deliverance from a situation that caused anxiety results in joy. The one who doesn't care about anything does not know the happiness of being relieved. But when worry becomes the fundamental driving force of someone's life, all joy disappears; such a person is a misery to himself and to all around him. It is often an empty life which is dominated by worry—for worry can make small matters large; it can fulfill a need for focus and direction in one's life. Therefore, when one problem is solved, the emptiness returns and another worry has to be found. Such a person is happy to be unhappy, and worried if she is not worried.

If worriers are not worried about the future, they worry about the past. They torment themselves about the bad things they did and about the good things that they left undone, so that their past becomes an unbearable load to them. Worrying about the past and worrying about the future have a similar result: they draw our attention away from the present. We should remember: we are only present in the present, and if it is dominated by the past or the future, life slips away from under us and we live a life of absence. Such a life, filled with missed opportunities, provides an abundance of material to worry about at the end of our lives.

Worry can therefore become more than an innocent shortcoming; it can be an enslaving sin. Like most sins, it is caused by a lack of love and humility. At the root of our worrying nature is pride, the unwillingness to bow before God and trust God with our lives, because *we* want to make the decisions. Instead of surrendering our lives to God, we stop halfway: we acknowledge, anxiously, that we're not masters of our own fate, but refuse to hand it over to the Lord. We are filled with fear, so that we have to be reminded of what John wrote: "There is no fear in love, but perfect love casts out fear" (1 John 4:18). If we love God and trust in God, fear is driven out, because trust cancels out fear.

A Positive Attitude

We are all afraid of poisonous snakes, but we often don't care about the poison of negative thoughts entering our minds and ruining our happiness. Unfortunately, it is easy to become so used to the thousands of good things that we daily receive that we take them for granted; whereas things that go wrong force themselves upon our attention. We are, in a manner of speaking, much more conscious of a painful toe than of the healthy state of the rest of the body. Therefore it takes an effort of the will to let positive thoughts enter our minds and restore our inner balance. We don't have to ignore our troubles, but we should not allow them to dominate our minds. Negative thoughts have a way of multiplying—if we let one in, a multitude of others follow. Someone who went through a deep depression said that she was gradually healed through a conscious, daily repeated decision to turn her "grey" thoughts into "pink" ones. She changed her habit of turning every experience into a negative thought into a habit of discovering positive facets in each situation.

Of course, not every depression can be cured by "pulling yourself together," by "looking on the bright side of things." There are depressions where chemical factors play a role, which need medication; there are depressions caused by deeply traumatic events that can only be worked through over a long period. But the healing process can be assisted by the changing of negative thought patterns, by the opening of oneself to positive possibilities, and by discovering the God whose love is steadfast during all seasons of life.

Compassionate Suffering

There is a dark side of life that we cannot help observing, and we should not either. We should not forget the warning that Oom Diederik received in his dream: if we are not filled with sadness by the sorrows and sins of the world, we have callous hearts. People with compassion have a sadness that moves them to change the world for the better: they act to alleviate the misery around them; they pray for those who suffer and sacrifice themselves for those in need. Paradoxically, their sadness also contains joy, for it gives them joy to help others and they are enriched by being connected to the world. Conversely, the one who shuts himself off from the needs of others gets isolated and his life becomes meaningless. So there is a sadness that leads to fulfillment and a gladness that is empty. The ideal is to be linked in love to others—sharing their sadness as well as their joy. More significant than sorrow or joy, in biblical ethics, is the experience of communion—of the oneness of the world and the interconnectedness of all.

Richard Foster explains how the "prayer of suffering" can help to alleviate the pain of others. He believes that this compassionate, suffering prayer has a redemptive element:

> In redemptive suffering we stand with people in their sin and in their sorrow. There can be no sterile, arm's-length

purity. Their suffering is a messy business and we must be prepared to step smack into the middle of the mess. We are "crucified" not just *for* others but also *with* others. We pray in suffering, and as we do, we are changed. Our hearts are enlarged to receive and accept all people. The language of "they" and "them" is converted into "we" and "us." All supposed superiority—whether intellectual, cultural or spiritual—simply melts away. Together we stand under the cross.

Joy, not misery, is the compelling energy behind redemptive suffering.[22]

For Foster the pain of suffering is linked to the joy of communion.

Foster tells a few stories that show how we can help people in misery through compassionate sadness—when we take their sorrow on us. He finds biblical examples of "redemptive suffering" in Moses, mediator between a righteous God and the sinful people of Israel, and in Jacob, wrestling all night with the angel. They are examples to us: we should also "refuse to let go until we receive a blessing—not for us, but for others. We argue with God so that his justice may be overcome by his mercy. It is only because of our intimacy with God that we can thus wrestle with him."[23] He even mentions the possibility of repenting on behalf of others, as Dietrich Bonhoeffer did for his Nazi enemies. Foster warns, however, that we should not try to take an unbearable load onto our shoulders: "We need not continue shouldering the burdens of others but rather we release them into the arms of the Father."[24]

In our compassionate suffering we are true followers of Christ, who was crucified to redeem a sinful world. In the story of the crucifixion we see how joy and sorrow are intertwined in the Christian faith. Golgotha is the source of our deepest sadness as well as our greatest joy; the suffering of the cross was followed by the glory of the resurrection. Thus we can see that the Christian faith does not proclaim a life of exclusive sadness or joy. In

---

22. Foster, *Prayer*, 232.
23. Ibid., 239.
24. Ibid., 237.

our daily life as Christians we echo the death and resurrection of Jesus, experiencing the painful death of the old self and the joyful breaking through of a new life. The ultimate aim of the Christian life is therefore not to look for joy by avoiding pain, nor to wallow in our sorrow and refuse to be consoled—both joy and sadness are contained in the ultimate virtue of love towards God and our fellow human beings.

Joy in Difficult Times

In the chapter on "Hope" I mentioned that the prophets foresaw light and darkness alternating in the future of Israel. Sometimes, in the history of nations, there are beautiful times of virtue and harmony, when leaders and followers are united in doing what is right. Such a time was during the first fully democratic elections in South Africa, in 1994, when justice was done and goodwill prevailed. A bit of heaven then breaks through to the earth; we experience the beauty of virtues like justice and kindness; we are reminded what the world should be like. But alas, such times do not last, a bit of hell—often more than a bit—reappears, and good people have to practice their virtue in adverse circumstances, where their mettle is tested. Heaven clearly does not have a permanent abode on earth; it only shows glimpses of its glory.

The pattern of alternating darkness and light not only emerges in the history of nations, but also in the life of individuals. When Jesus died on the cross, everything must have seemed lost to the disciples; but the crucifixion was followed by the resurrection and the ascension, and Luke tells us that the disciples "returned to Jerusalem with great joy; and they were continually in the temple blessing God" (Luke 24:52–53). A few weeks later the disciples were filled with the Holy Spirit; new converts were made, and it seemed that all was well now—the disciples "ate their food with glad and generous hearts, praising God and having the goodwill of all the people" (Acts 2:46–47). In the following chapters in Acts, however, we read about the troubles of the first disciples: Peter and John are brought before the Jewish Council because they claimed that Jesus had risen from the dead; Peter lands in jail; Stephen is stoned; James, the brother of John, is killed. The disciples' faith seemed to have brought them bad luck.

In the letter of James we find a surprising reaction to their hardships: "Whenever you face trials of any kind, consider it nothing but joy" (Jas 1:2). This seems crazy, to be glad about trials. In the following verse James gives his readers the reasons why they should accept their tribulations and even be glad about them: their faith has to be tested to see whether it is genuine, whether it will last under adverse circumstances. Only through hardship can the quality of their faith be determined, for if faith should bring prosperity, one could not be sure whether it is faith or prosperity that is the main attraction for believers. Furthermore, in hard times they can acquire endurance, a virtue that by definition can only develop in adversity. For James, having the virtues of Christianity was more important than having prosperity and good fortune.

In the first letter of Peter, similar reasons are given why the readers should not be despondent about their trials. Their suffering is necessary "so that the genuineness of your faith—being more precious than gold that, though perishable, is tested by fire—may be found to result in praise and glory and honor when Jesus Chris is revealed" (1 Pet 1:7). The genuineness of their faith is of prime importance, especially in the light of eternity. In the secular world, gold has a very high value, since it is so beautiful and lasts so long. For Peter, genuine faith is "more precious"—it has a spiritual beauty surpassing the splendor of gold, and it lasts to all eternity.

Like James, Peter suggests that they should be joyful, even under difficult circumstances. For him, the wonderful salvation brought about by Jesus is the greatest reason to be joyful. He mentions the resurrection of Jesus, which provided the possibility of "a new birth and a living hope"; they have "an inheritance that is imperishable, undefiled, and unfading, kept in heaven" (1:4). Therefore Peter encourages them to praise God, the "Father of our Lord Jesus Christ" (1:3). Through Peter we too are reminded that we should not take our salvation for granted; we should meditate on it, be gladdened by it, and praise God for it. In the practice of praising the Lord, much joy is created.

The idea of a joy lasting in all circumstances is not limited to the New Testament; we find a similar thought in the book of Habakkuk:

> Though the fig tree does not blossom,
> and no fruit is on the vines;
> though the produce of the olive fails,
> and the fields yield no food;
> though the flock is cut off from the fold,
> yet I will rejoice in the Lord;
> I will exult in the God of my salvation.
> God, the Lord, is my strength;
> He makes my feet like the feet of a deer,
> and makes me tread upon the heights. (3:17–19)

The joy that the prophet speaks about is independent of circumstances. Habakkuk lists some things that are vital in a farming community—the fig trees and the vineyards must produce fruit, the flocks must provide meat—and then considers what would happen to him if all these things were lacking: still he would rejoice in the Lord. One can be cynical and remark that if there is no food, there will soon be no prophet to rejoice. But the idea that Habakkuk wants to convey, is clear: God is to him more important than the material things on which most people set their minds. He does not focus on the harvest, but on the Lord from whom all blessings come, with whom he has a living relationship. Habakkuk rejoices "in the Lord," for he is united with God; he exults in the salvation of his God, who fulfills all his needs. Although each day contains its challenges, its "mountains," God grants him the strength to overcome—God makes his feet like those of a deer, so that he can ascend each height on his path. God is the foundation of all his joy.

JOY AND PEACE

Brother Lawrence and Mother Theresa

Continuing communion with God was the central theme of the spiritual classic *The Practice of the Presence of God*, by Brother Lawrence. Brother Lawrence, who became a lay brother in a Carmelite monastery during the seventeenth century, had to work in a hospital kitchen—a job he hated. But he found a way of keeping his calm: "You need to accustom yourself to continual conversation with God—a conversation which is free and simple. . . . As we go about this pursuit we should simply offer all things to Him before we do them and give Him thanks when we have finished."[25]

The life of Brother Lawrence was one of continuing prayer. He writes: "The time of business . . . does not differ with me from the time of prayer; and in the noise and clatter of my kitchen, while several persons are at the same time calling for different things, I possess God in as great a tranquility as if I were upon my knees at the blessed sacrament."[26] Brother Lawrence had accustomed himself to doing everything in that kitchen, everything in life for the love of God.

However, there are saintly people who do not always experience the peace of God's presence; Mother Theresa of Calcutta is a prime example. She had a strong sense of being called by Jesus to devote herself to him, but after a few years she lost that consciousness of the presence of God which Brother Lawrence valued so highly. She "experienced some of the dreadful reality of a life without God, which she likened to hell, the consequence of the ultimate rejection of his love and his mercy."[27] For many years she was deeply troubled by the painful feeling of isolation, but she was comforted by her spiritual adviser, Father Neuner, who assured her that there was no serious failure on her part that could explain the "spiritual dryness." He said: "It was simply the dark night of which all masters of spiritual life know. . . . Thus the only response

---

25. Bother Lawrence, *Practicing His Presence*, 55.
26. Ibid., 103.
27. Kolodiejchuk, *Mother Theresa*, 250.

to this trial is the total surrender to God and the acceptance of the darkness in union with Jesus."[28]

Mother Theresa's pain was an example of the redemptive suffering, suffering for the sake of others: "This experience fueled her unquenchable thirst to save souls by helping each person to know God and his love, and to love Him in return. Along with her whole-hearted service to the poor, she was offering to God her hidden agony so that others could draw close to Him."[29] She realized that, in her loneliness, she was sharing in the suffering of her Savior. She wrote to her fellow workers: "At the Incarnation Jesus became like us in all things except sin; but at the time of the Passion, He became sin. He took on our sins and that was why He was rejected by the Father. . . . Do you realize that when you accept the vows you accept the same fate as Jesus?"[30]

So, although the uninterrupted communion with God that Brother Lawrence experienced—the source of unending joy—still remains an ideal for us, the truth of the matter is that many believers go through times when they feel far from God. There could be many reasons for this feeling, but it is not necessarily a sign of sin. If we are not conscious of a sin that we cling to and that separates us from God, we should, like Mother Theresa, offer the "hidden agony" to God, to be used in God's service.

Angry with God

Most of us have had times when we were angry with God; our anger left no room for joy. We may have been angered by the terrible things that God allows to happen, as Job was. Theresa of Avila reproached God in her adversities, saying: if this is the way you treat your friends, it's no wonder you have so few! When bad things happen, we wonder: Where is the God who is supposed to be caring? Where is the God of justice when injustice prevails? Where

---

28. Ibid., 214.
29. Ibid., 250.
30. Ibid., 250–51.

is the "Almighty" when good people are unprotected against the assaults of the wicked?

The psalms are full of reproachful calls to God. We read in the first verse of Psalm 74: "O God, why do you cast us off forever? Why does your anger smoke against the sheep of your pasture?" And in Psalm 88:14–16 we read: "O Lord, why do you cast me off? Why do you hide your face from me? . . . Your wrath has swept over me; your dread assaults destroy me." Like Theresa of Avila, the psalmists could not understand why God was so hard on people of the covenant. We have also discussed the anger of Job towards God, caused by what Job perceived to be God's unjust treatment of one who served God faithfully. We mentioned that the kind of anger which Job showed was actually pleasing to God. It was a sign that he cared, that he wanted justice to prevail.

Many answers have been given to the great question of why God allows bad things to happen to good people. However, ultimately we have to acknowledge that we cannot understand the reasons for all the suffering of the world, we cannot comprehend the fickleness and cruelty of fate, and we cannot fully answer the age-old question: if God is good and almighty, why does God allow so many terrible things to happen? Like Job, we may vent our anger to God, but like Job we should ultimately admit the limitations of our knowledge and our understanding, and realize that we cannot argue with God on an equal footing. Events that baffle us also remind us that we cannot put God into a little box to be analyzed; the one who "understands" God clearly does not know God. The theologian Paul Tillich goes so far as to say: "A god whom we can easily bear, a god from whom we do not have to hide, a god whom we do not hate in moments, a god whose destruction we never desire, is not God at all, and has no reality."[31]

As mentioned before, God responded to all the questions about the inexplicable suffering in the world with only one word of consolation—the Word who became flesh. As Christians we are enormously consoled by God's incarnation in Jesus, the "reflection of God's glory and the exact imprint of God's very being" (Heb

---

31. Tillich, "Escape from God."

1:3). We can be angry with God, but it is hard to be angry with Jesus, through whom the limitless love of God towards the world was revealed. Through Jesus God revealed to us what we, limited human beings, can digest (and even Jesus is far more than we can comprehend!); but if we had to be shown the totality of God's Being, we would not be able to endure it. Moses wanted to see the full glory of God, and was reminded: "You cannot see my face; for no one shall see me and live" (Exod 33:20). So Moses was only granted to see the back of God (Exod 33:23). Jesus revealed, as it were, the heart, but not the whole Being of God—the earth could not contain God's fullness, and we could not bear it. We should not try to comprehend God; but we can meditate on what was revealed of God in Jesus, and be consoled and gladdened by it.

The Death of God

In a situation of severe trauma, it may seem to us that God dies in our hearts and minds. Elie Wiesel had such an experience. From early childhood he studied the Talmud and worshipped God. But then, in Auschwitz, when he saw the smoke curling from the furnace into which his mother and his sister and many other victims had been thrown, his old life fell apart.

> Never shall I forget that night, the first night in the camp, that turned my life into one long night seven times sealed.
>
> Never shall I forget that smoke.
>
> Never shall I forget the small faces of the children whose bodies I saw transformed into smoke under a silent sky.
>
> Never shall I forget the nocturnal silence that deprived me for all eternity of the desire to live.
>
> Never shall I forget those moments that murdered my God and my soul and turned my dreams to ashes.
>
> Never shall I forget those things, even were I condemned to live as long as God Himself.
>
> Never.[32]

32. Wiesel, *Night*, 34.

Joy and Peace

The foreword for *Night* was written by Francois Mauriac, a French writer and a Christian, to whom Elie Wiesel showed his manuscript. In the foreword Mauriac recalls a horrible scene in the book where Wiesel, a mere child, witnessed the hanging of another child who "had the face of an angel." Wiesel heard someone groan behind him: "For God's sake, where is God?" And he heard from within him a voice reply: "Where is he? This is where—hanging here from this gallows."[33] Mauriac is deeply moved and comments:

> And I, who believe that God is love, what answer was there to give my young interlocutor whose dark eyes still held the reflection of the angelic sadness that had appeared one day on the face of a hanged child? What did I say to him? Did I speak to him of that other Jew, this crucified brother who perhaps resembled him and whose cross conquered the world? Did I explain to him that what had been a stumbling block for *his* faith had become a cornerstone for *mine*? And that the connection between the cross and the human suffering remains, in my view, the key to the unfathomable mystery in which the faith of his childhood was lost?[34]

Considering the "unfathomable mystery" of the suffering of Auschwitz, Mauriac finds consolation in linking it to the "cornerstone" of his faith: the suffering and conquering God, as revealed by his Son Jesus Christ in his crucifixion and resurrection. Mauriac believes that the God whom Wiesel worshipped as a child is also the God who died on the cross. The God of Christians is not a distant, callous Being, but a suffering God filled with compassion. This is a truth to meditate upon, with deep sadness and great joy.

The poems of Geoffrey Studdert Kennedy, an Anglican pastor who served in the First World War, movingly express his emotions and thoughts in a time of great suffering. He too found consolation in the thought of God sharing our suffering. I quote a few lines from his poem "The Suffering God":

> Father, if He, the Christ were Thy Revealer,

33. Ibid., xx.
34. Ibid., xxi.

Truly the First Begotten of the Lord,
Then must Thou be a Suff'rer and a Healer,
Pierced to the heart by the sorrow of the sword.
Then must it mean, not only that Thy sorrow
Smote Thee that once upon the lonely tree,
But that to-day, to-night, and on the morrow,
Still it will come, O Gallant God, to Thee.[35]

Jesus, Our Example and Our Savior

This brings us to a theme that runs like a refrain through all the chapters of the book: Jesus, our example and our Savior. Let us then meditate on the joy of Jesus. In contrast with John the Baptist, Jesus was not an ascetic. He loved food and wine and the company of friends—no wonder the Pharisees reproached him, saying: "Look, a glutton and a drunkard, a friend of tax collectors and sinners" (Matt 11:19). When he spoke about the kingdom of God, he compared it to a banquet with plenty of food (22:4). Furthermore, in the Sermon on the Mount, we see how much he appreciated the wonder and beauty of nature: "Consider the lilies of the field, how they grow; they neither toil nor spin, yet I tell you, even Solomon in all his glory was not clothed like one of these" (6:28–29).

Although Jesus loved the good things of the earth—the beauty of nature, good food and wine, and the company of friends—he did not cling to life when his time had come. He led his life in accordance with the will of his beloved God and was willing to die when his task was finished. Therefore he knew the deep joy of fulfillment, for he had finished the work that God gave him to do (John 17:4). It is significant that, in John's Gospel, Jesus talks about his joy on the eve of his crucifixion (15:11)—clearly his joy transcended his tragic circumstances. A part of this joy was caused by the prospect of being eternally united with his Father (14:28)—a joy that he had already partly tasted on earth, the joy of constant communion with God. Jesus says that even

---

35. Studdert Kennedy, *Unutterable Beauty*, 13.

when his disciples will be scattered and leave him alone, he will not be completely alone, "because the Father is with me" (16:32).

Joy and Peace

In his last conversations with his disciples, as recorded in John, Jesus speaks about his joy, but more often about his peace. For instance: "I have said this to you, so that in me you may have peace. In the world you face persecution. But take courage; I have conquered the world" (John 16:33). There is a marked contrast between "in the world" and "in me"—in the world they will be prosecuted, whereas in communion with Jesus they will have peace. Jesus has withstood the demands of the world, the temptations of Satan, and even the human desire to avoid the suffering of the cross. He has received the perfect peace of someone in total harmony with God, and that is the peace he wants his disciples to inherit from him: "Peace I leave with you; my peace I give to you. I do not give to you as the world gives. Do not let your hearts be troubled, and do not let them be afraid" (14:27).

The peace of the world is different from the peace that Jesus grants. In the world, we call it peace when there is no war; but very often the wars in our hearts continue after the violence of physical war has ended. The peace of Jesus is an inner peace that fills our troubled hearts and drives out inner turmoil. It is a peace that the world cannot give and that his disciples cannot attain on their own; but Jesus has conquered and they will be conquerors too—by taking Jesus as their example and by allowing the Holy Spirit, who is to come, to bring the abundance of Jesus to fruition in their lives (14:26).

Maybe we should think of *joy* as a component of the more comprehensive notion of *peace*. Although the meanings of these two words partly overlap, people tend to link joy to a joyous occurrence, whereas peace is less dependent on circumstances; it is a more inclusive concept, more than an emotional reaction to good news; it encompasses joy as well as its opposite, sorrow. The foundation of the Christian's joy is the good news of Golgotha:

forgiveness and victory over sin and death. That event provided the basis for a lasting peace and inner wholeness. Peace is linked to harmony—inner harmony as well as harmony with our fellow human beings. Above all, it is obtained by living in harmony with God, by obeying God's commands and trusting God to take care of our lives. It is the sublime peace of which Paul wrote: "And the peace of God, which passes all understanding, will guard your hearts and your minds in Christ Jesus" (Phil 4:7).

6

Truth

What Is Truth?

"What is truth?" Pilate asked Jesus (John 18:38). This was his skeptical response to what Jesus had said to him a moment before: "For this I was born, and for this I came into the world, to testify to the truth. Everyone who belongs to the truth listens to my voice." One can have some sympathy with the governor—he had to deal with so many different claims to the truth. Those fanatic Jews claimed that Jesus called himself the king of the Jews and thus challenged the power of the emperor and endangered the peace in Israel. However, Jesus denied that he wanted to establish a kingdom on earth, but then proclaimed that he was indeed a king—a king revealing *the* truth, mind you. Pilate was aware of the many nations ruled by the Romans; he must have known that they were all adherents of their own truths. And then there were also the conflicting voices within one nation, as he experienced in Israel—no wonder the Roman governor reacted with skepticism to Jesus' words, which must have sounded both naive and arrogant to him.

Today many people would sympathize with Pilate's attitude. For who can answer the question: what is truth? There are so many definitions of truth: people talk about *historical truth* when a statement corresponds with the facts; but also about *meaningful truth* when something makes sense to them; about *pragmatic truth* when a belief is useful though it cannot be proven; about *psychological truth* when a statement is the expression of a genuine inner experience, even if it is not factually true; and so forth. Apart from the different definitions, people's versions of the truth differ according to their personalities and experience. So often people regard their little truths as absolute, and despise and make war on people with a different "truth." The real problem seems to be the people who think they can answer the question "What is truth?"—not the intellectual problem posed by the question.

We all know, or should know, that the concept of truth is subjective. Apart from the fact that our views are determined by our individual personalities and experience, we must also bear in mind that we experience the world subjectively through our senses—for a horse or a fly, the world would look different from what it looks to us, because their sensual organs differ from ours. Our bodies are used as criterion when we describe the world—what is bigger than us we call big, what is smaller we call small. What deviates from the general norm we call ugly—we would not like the sight, for instance, of people with two noses and three eyes. There is no place to be found from where we could observe the world objectively, where we could have a "God's eye" view. So is it not clear that what we call "*the* truth" is based on a thoroughly human, personal view of reality? Surely *the* truth cannot fit into a modern person's vocabulary?

I Am the Truth

As in many other respects, Jesus brings a radical reinterpretation of "the truth." He confirms that the truth is subjective—but subjective in a surprising way. What Pilate would not have known is that Jesus, at another time, made an even stranger statement about the truth when he said: "I am the truth" (John 14:6). What on earth could that mean? One speaks the truth, one *is* not the truth. This statement leads us to an astounding conclusion: that the ultimate truth is not a statement, but a Person, a Person in a loving relationship with the world. Jesus, the Son of God, revealed the caring heart of his heavenly Creator; the greatest truth revealed by Jesus is God's love for God's creation. That means that there is truly no such thing as objective reality, for behind the objective reality of the world is a subjective Creator longing to enter into a relationship of love with the world.

Little did Pilate know that the truth Jesus was speaking about was standing right in front of him. The truth embodied in the person of Jesus was revealed in a narrative, in a history played out at a specific time in a specific place, with Jesus as the main character. Many other characters formed part of the story: his disciples, the crowd who demanded his crucifixion, Pilate himself as well. The story contains many aspects of the truth of God's relationship with the world, for instance: the aversion to uncontaminated goodness, as revealed by the crowd who demanded the death of a virtuous man; the lack of courage shown by the disciples in a time of crisis, when they ran away as Jesus was arrested; the cowardice of Peter and the treachery of Judas, who denied and betrayed their Master, respectively; and, in sharp contrast, the boundless love of Jesus, which led him to sacrifice himself for the sake of the world. It is the history of a relationship—it reveals, on the one hand, the human need of salvation and, on the other hand, God's eagerness to provide it. The crucifixion of Jesus, the image of his Creator, reveals the extent of God's love; the resurrection reveals the extent of God's power; the outpouring of the Holy Spirit reveals God's dramatic entry into the hearts of the disciples and God's transforming power in their lives. This is the true story of which Pilate knew nothing; in Jesus' words, it is a truth to which (to whom) Pilate did not belong.

On another occasion Jesus used words, incomprehensible to some of his disciples, that revealed a different aspect of "the truth." He said: "Those who eat my flesh and drink my blood have eternal life, and I will raise them up on the last day; for my flesh is true food and my blood is true drink" (John 6:54, 55). This image suggests an intimate relationship between Jesus and his disciples, for what we eat and drink becomes part of our bodies: "Those who eat my flesh and drink my blood abide in me, and I in them" (6:56). For those who "eat his flesh," Jesus is always present in their lives, and they remind themselves continually of that presence, as Brother Lawrence did. They strive to do his will in every situation and they wait on him to provide what they need. Food and drink keep us alive physically; similarly, the flesh and blood of Jesus, symbolizing his sacrifice on Golgotha, keep us spiritually alive, so that we can hear God's voice, obey God's commands, and enjoy God's presence. These verses indicate that the truth of Jesus is not discerned from an "objective distance"—he works out his will in the lives of his disciples in an intimate, mystical union with them. Christians become imitators of Christ—as Thomas á Kempis put it, people of his mind—followers of Jesus in whom God's love is incarnated once again. His flesh is indeed "true food," his blood "true drink."

Subjective Relativism?

The claim stated above, that the truth is subjective, needs to be qualified. It does not mean that "anything goes," that each person has his own subjective truth, and that we cannot argue about the question whether or not a statement or a belief is factually true. Such a position would lead to a quite untenable relativism. In court, everyone's "subjective truth" would have to be accepted; there would be no way of determining what evidence is reliable and what not. There would be no liars anymore, and no one would speak the truth.

Our subjectivity does not mean that the objects about which we form our conceptions are not real, and that statements cannot be checked for their reliability. Perhaps it would be better to formulate the situation in this way: there is an objective reality which each of us experiences subjectively. The world in which we live is real; it is not a figment of the imagination; but it finds its most fundamental meaning, its final truth, in the relationship of the creation with its Creator. It is a relationship of love, revealed by the coming of Jesus into the world.

From this "final truth," the fundamental relationship between Creator and creation, flows another truth: we as humans are connected to each other, and we are all connected to the natural world.

We all have a common Source, a God of love who has commanded us to care for each other and for the world we live in. Responsible for each other, dependent on each other, we proclaim the unity of the world created by our Creator, who is One. No one is alone in the world.

The Only Way?

We should now have a look at the full statement of Jesus when he declared himself to be "the truth." It is a statement that has been problematic to many people: "I am the way, and the truth, and the life. No one comes to the Father except through me" (John 14:6). The truth that Jesus proclaimed is that he is the way—the only way—to God and to eternal life. Does that mean that all who do not follow Jesus are eternally damned?

The Bible as a whole does not see the matter in such a simplistic way. It is clear that many of the characters in the Old Testament experienced a close communion with God, long before the coming of Christ. We find it in many psalms—in Psalm 51 for instance, where David expresses his intense remorse about his relationship with Bathsheba and his great fear that he may lose the experience of the presence of God as a result of his sins. Therefore he pleads to God: "Do not cast me away from your presence, and do not take your holy spirit away from me" (v. 11). Although the psalmist could not know the full richness of the message of Jesus, he lived in the blessedness of God's presence and with the knowledge of God's Holy Spirit long before Jesus revealed himself as the way to God.

Furthermore, we have to acknowledge that some people outside the Christian tradition—people like Socrates and Gandhi—have shown much more of a likeness to Christ than most people within the Christian tradition. The wisdom of Socrates has been a respected guide in the development of Western philosophy over the centuries; Gandhi, through his struggle against oppression and his rejection of violence, is still an inspirational example to millions. Both these virtuous men were killed, like Christ, as a result of their adherence to their high ethical ideals. Are they lost because they did not know the way and the truth that Jesus revealed?

These are questions that no person can answer confidently—only God can judge people with total righteousness and grace. But we may venture a few suggestions. We have all experienced in a good film, drama, or literary narrative that every scene is connected to what has gone before and what comes thereafter. For Christians, Jesus takes a central position in the history of God's relationship with the world. In God's universal narrative, the great moral teachers of the world echo the teachings of the main character, Jesus Christ. But people outside the Christian tradition also form part of God's narrative. Many of them also acknowledge their need of the grace of God and strive to be virtuous—more than they know, they are linked to the narrative in which Christians believe. Socrates could be regarded as a prefiguration of Jesus, Gandhi as a reminder of the values for which he stood.

Non-Christians who adhere to the values of Christ would feel at home with him in the life hereafter; to evil people he would be a threat and an enemy. He will still divide people, as he did on earth. We as Christians, by following the example of Jesus as portrayed in the Gospels, by spreading the grace and charity of Christ through the world, could attract people outside the church to the glory of Jesus, even without converting them to Christianity, without them realizing whom they meet through us. The grace of God works in mysterious ways.

Through the sacrifice of Jesus, Christians believe, the righteous wrath of God was averted—God's anger not only towards Israel, but towards the whole world—and it was converted into an overwhelming grace. From the cross of Jesus flows a benevolence to all, and, in more ways than we can imagine, God speaks to the world, revealing his values and wishes. Indeed, as the apostle John wrote, Jesus "is the atoning sacrifice for our sins, and not for ours only but also for the sins of the whole world" (1 John 2:2). Everyone will answer for his own response to the manifold voices of God.

Truly Faithful

There is another aspect of the truth that we should consider. In English, one talks about a "true statement" as well as a "true friend." These two meanings of "true" are different, but also connected. The Hebrew *emeth*, corresponding to English "truth," is often used in the Old Testament to describe God. Not only his words are true; his Person is also trustworthy. A true friend is one in whom we can have faith; she is trustworthy. The Pharisees were the opposite: they were totally false, "like whitewashed tombs, which on the outside look beautiful, but inside they are full of the bones of the dead and of all kinds of filth" (Matt 23:27). Jesus was true because he was transparent; he was what he said he was. He called himself the good shepherd: "I am the good shepherd. The good shepherd lays down his life for the sheep" (John 10:11); and he proved the truth of his statement by being true unto death.

Being true is being sincere as well as being faithful. It means that there is no contrast between outward pretense and innermost being; it also means that one is true to one's word. A true person is an honest person who doesn't have to hide her actions, because there is nothing to be ashamed of; she is not treacherous, but remains steadfast to the end. In all these respects, Jesus was true; and he wanted to make his disciples true as he was—honest, sincere, faithful, and trustworthy. In that process he had to rid them of their illusions, especially of the untruth that they were by nature true friends of their Master. Peter vehemently declared that he would never deny Jesus, and yet he did just that very soon afterwards. Peter had to look deep into his undependable heart and shed bitter tears before the Holy Spirit could transform him into a truly trustworthy disciple—one who spoke courageously when the Jewish Council tried to prevent him from proclaiming the resurrection of Jesus (Acts 4:19, 20), whose life ended in martyrdom (John 21:18, 19)—according to tradition, on a cross like his Savior. The disciple who once denied Jesus became firm as a rock.

Blind to the Truth

"Love is blind," goes the saying; but it is not true—certainly not about the love of which the Bible speaks. It is infatuation that makes people blind, that leads them to irrational decisions—indeed, infatuation often makes a fool of us. Self-centeredness also blinds us to the reality around us. Biblical love, in contrast, makes us clear-sighted.

Paul is harsh in his criticism of the senselessness of his times:

> Ever since the creation of the world his eternal power and divine nature, invisible though they are, have been understood and seen through the things he has made. So they are without excuse; for though they knew God, they did not honor him as God or give thanks to him, but they became futile in their thinking, and their senseless minds were darkened. Claiming to be wise, they became foolish. (Rom 1:20–22)

The greatness of God, Paul claims, can be deduced from God's creation, but people have separated creation from its Creator. Is that not true of our times as well? In our pride, we have lost the ability to stand in awe before a Creator whose power and intelligence is clearly infinitely greater than ours. We rationalize and invent clever-sounding theories about a world that could have come into existence without outside influence—not because our theories are plausible, but because the idea of a Creator makes us uncomfortable. We have missed the central truth of the creation: the glory of the Creator.

We don't take in the miraculous in everyday life: the sun rising and setting regularly, the succession of seasons, the birth of a child—all the wonderful things in creation of which God reminded Job (Job 38–41). Although these events are determined by natural laws of cause and effect, the laws are in themselves miraculous, and their ultimate Cause cannot be explained. But rationalism provides a reassuring escape; it provides an easy solution: just ban from your consciousness the things that you cannot explain, so that you don't have to bow before a Power whom you cannot comprehend.

If we had to seriously consider the testimony of the disciples that Jesus was resurrected, it would make unbearable demands on our lives. So we rather put the story into the category of fairy tale, and file it away safely. In various ways the Holy Spirit speaks to us—through nature, through the Bible, through our circumstances, through the silent voice from deep inside. But we tend to rush from one commitment to the next to silence that voice which we find disturbing. So we miss the message that the Spirit wants to convey: the truth of God inviting us into a relationship with our Creator.

We are also often blind to the truth of the people around us. We distort the world; we don't see others in their own right, but regard them as objects to be used. In our narcissism, using ourselves as criterion, we stereotype those who are different; we put them into a little box where we keep them imprisoned. Since we fail to consider the possibility of change in them, we do nothing to help them realize their potential.

Furthermore, we often fail to respond to those in need. The need may be obvious or not so obvious—someone may have a deep need and does not dare to reveal it explicitly—but if we would listen attentively to the truth behind the words, we would be able to understand and respond appropriately. We hear about the many needs of the world—poverty and sickness, trauma and death are all around us; and we become despondent, concluding that there are too many problems for us to solve—and then we do nothing. We don't notice the things we can do to bring relief.

It is clear that there is a close connection between love and truth on the one hand, and between pride and self-deception on the other. This applies to our relationship with God as well as our relationship with other people. In our pride, we have illusions of grandeur about ourselves and refuse to bow before God. In humility, in contrast, we discover the greatness of God and respond with wonder and awe to God's calling. In our self-centeredness the reality of people needing us passes us by; whereas love makes us sensitive viewers and listeners, enables us to see the potential in others and notice their needs. Without love we are like living corpses, unconscious of the most important truths in the world. And it is only the Spirit of truth (John 14:17), who is also the Spirit of love (Rom 5:5), that can open our eyes to the truth and fill us with love.

Creating the Truth

Truth is not only something to be discovered, but also something to be created. "According to your faith let it be done to you," Jesus said to the blind men (Matt 9:29). They believed, and were healed; their faith created the possibility to be healed. Every person, through his attitude, shapes his world. "Every mind constructs its world, and as the mind, so the world," wrote the philosopher Marthinus Versfeld.[36] And according to the way we construct the world, we act. Those who have faith in God allow God to enter their lives and transform them, through them God changes the world for the better. Indeed, the hope of the world lies with those who have the faith to imagine a better world and the courage to act according to their faith.

Conversely, those who are evil break down what good people build. Cynical people spread their lies wherever they go; they proclaim that the world cannot be changed. Therefore they refrain from action and leave everything as it is—or rather, they make things worse, for they destroy prospects of improvement wherever they go. In the cosmic battle portrayed in the Bible, Satan is the "father of lies" (John 8:44); he denies the truth of the abundant life that God provides in Jesus. Satan is a nihilist, a thief who "comes only to steal and kill and destroy"(10:10); Jesus offers new possibilities for those who believe, and through them for the people around them. In the great battle between the Creator and the Nihilist, we are all involved.

---

36. Versfeld, *Our Selves*, 20.

The Truth Will Make You Free

We have often argued, in the preceding chapters, how Christian values are linked to each other. Truth, too, is not an isolated concept; Jesus linked truth to freedom when he told his disciples: "You will know the truth, and the truth will make you free" (John 8:32). The disciples were puzzled by this statement and declared that they, as descendants of Abraham, had never been slaves. They associated slavery with working conditions and political power; Jesus had something else in mind: "Very truly, I tell you, everyone who commits sin is a slave to sin" (8:34). Sin enslaves in more than one sense—it leads us to do what we know we shouldn't do, and to feelings of guilt as a result of that. Paul describes this kind of slavery well in Romans 7:21–24:

> So I find it to be a law that when I want to do what is good, evil lies close at hand. For I delight in the law of God in my inmost self, but I see in my members another law at war with the law of my mind, making me captive to the law of sin that dwells in my members. Wretched man that I am! Who will rescue me from this body of death?

The word "law" is used in a number of different ways here; each meaning expresses a different aspect of the truth that can make us free. The word contains the meaning of "commandment," as well as of "necessity," as in a law of nature. In the first place, says Paul, there is the law of God, given to Moses—a law of moral prescriptions with which Paul can identify; to him it has become "the law of my mind." But, in conflict with the law of God which Paul has internalized, another law enters the picture: the law of natural desires, a law with its own demands—demands that are so strong that the law of God is overthrown. So a third law emerges with its own necessity: the law of the inevitable result of disobedience to the law of God—feelings of failure and guilt.

The truth that Paul identifies here is that the more virtuous one tries to be, the stronger the inner reaction against the attempted virtue becomes. The higher we aim to fly, the harder we fall; the stronger our resistance to inner evil, the more powerful the "enemy" gets. Knowing that something is wrong often makes the temptation more luring. Is there any solution to this dilemma of failing to do what we ought to, of not being what we should be? Must we stop trying so hard to be virtuous, and settle for half-hearted goodness? Paul offers a different solution: "Thanks be to God through Jesus Christ our Lord!" (Rom 7:24).

In Romans 8 Paul explains the gospel's liberating truth, the solution for this inner dilemma. The gospel proclaims a way of life where "there is no condemnation" (v. 1), no place for guilt feelings, because the followers of Christ have been justified (v. 33); nothing, not even their continual failings, can separate them from the love of God anymore (vv. 38–39). A fourth law now comes to the fore: a law of the Spirit (v. 2). This law also contains a necessity, similar to the law of failure explained in Romans 7, but with a vast difference—it is the necessity of the loving care of God. This is not a foreboding law, but a liberating one; it creates love by loving. The children of God are led out of bondage into a life of peace (v. 6); they are not slaves any more, but children of God; they have nothing to fear (v. 15). They are heirs of God who will be glorified (v. 17)—glorified with the nature of Christ, with something of his beauty reflected in them, through the working of his Spirit.

This liberation by Christ is beautifully prefigured in the last book of the Old Testament: "But for you who revere my name the sun of righteousness shall rise, with healing in its wings. You shall go out leaping like calves from the stall" (Mal 4:2). The text points to the coming of Christ, the sun of righteousness, whose rays would shine on his followers—healing them from the ill effects of sin and guilt, filling them with the exuberance of liberated people. The joyful calves in Malachi remind us of an image that Jesus used: "I am the gate. Whoever enters by me will be saved, and will come in and go out and find pasture. . . . I came that they may have life, and have it abundantly" (John 10:9–10). Through Jesus, the door, the cattle are free to go in and out—into the stall for protection in the night, and out into the pastures where food is plentiful. It is the joyful freedom of being protected from evil as well the freedom to go into the world, sustained and strengthened by food in abundance.

Unkind Truths

Truth is linked to freedom; but there are truths that do not liberate. There are truths that are unkind: we can hurt people by pointing out their faults to them too bluntly—faults of which they could well be conscious and which bother them as well. Of course, situations may arise where we have to point out their mistakes and wrongs to others; our truth may then be liberating to them. The important question is: what is our motivation in telling the truth? Are we moved by anger or by love? Do we want to hurt or to help?

Traumatic memories may sometimes be so unbearable that the survivors of trauma suppress them into their subconscious minds. It may not be beneficial to remind them what happened; it may be too much to bear. Furthermore, the historical truth about groups and nations and their past interaction often contains so much that is shameful that repeated reminders of the guilt of the past could destroy group relations, would result in a futile series of accusations and denials. Ultimately the truth has to come out, but we need to reveal it with humility, grace, and understanding. Truth is linked to, but subordinate to, love.

Political Freedom

Is the gospel only about inner freedom, and does it have nothing to say about political freedom? Does the fact that Jesus did not chase away the Romans mean that we should accept political injustice and bear that burden in peace? The question of political freedom is linked to the topic of justice, which was discussed in the chapter "Righteousness Etc." There we mentioned the vital importance of striving for a just society. We distinguished between personal anger and impartial justice, and mentioned that impartial justice is a value that is fundamental in Christian ethics. We also mentioned that the Christian struggle for human rights is different from the secular demand for human rights—the Christian's actions originate in the grace of God and acknowledge the responsibility of spreading the grace received.

An oppressive system is deeply detrimental to the oppressed, not only through the denial of their rights, but also through the low self-esteem it installs in them. Ultimately, as was mentioned in the chapter on "Righteousness Etc.," unrighteousness is also deeply harmful to the oppressor, whose humanity is lost when his sense of values is destroyed. So every caring person is obliged to oppose an oppressive, unjust system, and also, in a not completely evil system, to oppose aspects of the system that are oppressive and unjust. A society that is half-bad can so easily become totally corrupt if left alone.

The Freedom of Jesus

We have linked truth to freedom, and freedom to responsibility. So it is clear that the freedom discussed in this chapter is not only the freedom of joyfully liberated calves, which we mentioned above—that as well, but more than that. It is an inner solidity and wholeness: wanting to do what we should do, desiring to be what we ought to. It is a freedom that involves pain—like Jesus, we sometimes have to do what we find difficult; we may have to go against popular demand. It is the freedom of total surrender to God, a surrender that inevitably involves a cross.

The ultimate freedom of Jesus was revealed in an extremely painful way. According to the Gospel of Luke, the last words of Jesus before he died were: "Father, into your hands I commend my spirit" (Luke 23:46). The words of the dying Jesus in Luke echo the words of Psalm 31:5: "Into your hands I commit my spirit." These words in the psalm are preceded by the request to God to save the psalmist from the net that has been set for him, and are followed by the reassuring reminder: "You have redeemed me, O Lord, faithful God." So the psalmist's surrender is expressed within a context of trust in God; he can surrender his life to God because God is faithful.

Similarly, the last words of Jesus reveal his total trust in God. God has helped him right through his life—granted him power to heal, wisdom to preach his sermons, and strength to follow the way of the cross; God will also help him in his last moments—will receive his spirit and guide him into eternity. Significantly, Jesus adds one word to his quote from the psalm: "Father"—it was probably the intimate Aramaic *abba*, close in meaning to "daddy." It is the lifelong intimate relationship with his "Abba" that is the foundation of Jesus' trust in his heavenly Father. The truth of God's trustworthiness made Jesus free to do what is right, to be true till the end.

Jesus' total freedom was based on this total trust in God. There was no half-heartedness in his obedience; he was completely free to do what he knew was right. He was true unto death, true to his God, true to a world in need of salvation. And as Jesus was true, so was his God; the trust of Jesus was rewarded with eternal glory. The virtues of truth, freedom, faith, and joy are intertwined in his Person.

None of us can acquire the complete truth and freedom of Jesus—we dare not even aspire to it. His cross is scary; we would rather give up glory attained in such a horrible way. Yet the kingdom of God also has a place for ordinary citizens. To come too close to the sun would destroy us; but in our imperfect world, pieces of a broken mirror may reflect a bit of the brightness of the sun.

7

Love

The Central Message of the Bible

IF I HAD TO choose one text in the Bible that conveys the central message of the book, I would choose 1 John 4:16: "So we have known and believe the love that God has for us. God is love, and those who abide in love abide in God, and God abides in them."

The text indicates that biblical salvation originates in the love of God—love that was revealed in the coming of Jesus, the incarnation of God, into the world. In the suffering of Jesus, God suffered too, showing how much God cares for us and how highly God values us. We love because we have been loved; we cannot create heavenly love by ourselves. Yet we can respond to it and be transformed by it. Jesus is our example of how we should live; he is also our Savior who offers us the gift of transformative love. Through Jesus, the incarnation of God, heaven entered the earth; the kingdom of godly love was established.

The appropriate response to the love of God, as revealed in the life and death of Jesus, is to return God's love. We should be filled with wonder and gratitude by the fact that the God of the vast universe cares for us and suffers with us, minute creatures though we are; that this God has been faithful to us—in Jesus, unto death. We should also look with the love of God at ourselves, realizing our worth because God values us so greatly; we should furthermore look "through God's eyes" at the world, filled with God's love and care. When Jesus was born in a manger, the world received a new dignity—it was deemed worthy to be the dwelling of the incarnate God. We should therefore look at the whole world—humans, animals, and plants—with God's care and respect.

God is not only an example, our text proclaims; God wants to live in us, to reveal in us and through us God's limitless love, which proved itself by the great sacrifice on Golgotha. "God is love," our text proclaims. The essence of the Being of God—the most fundamental force in the universe—is love; and if we want to know God, we must abide in God; and if we abide in God, we have to abide in God's love as revealed through Jesus. There is no possibility of being united with God and being lacking in love. The heart of the message of the Bible is a life of love, lived in unity with God, who is Love.

Jesus also stressed the centrality of love when he responded to the lawyer's question about the greatest commandment. He said: "You shall love the Lord your God with all your heart, and with all your soul, and with all your mind. This is the greatest and first commandment. And a second is like it: You shall love your neighbor as yourself" (Matt 22:36-39). The first commandment given by Jesus is to love God with an undivided love, with our whole being—not merely with a love centered in the emotions or the mind. Jesus also indicates that our love towards God should be accompanied by love towards other people and towards ourselves. He leaves us no option for a love that is either vertical, focused on God, or horizontal, focused on other people or on ourselves. In his ethics, to love God means to love God's creation, and loving the creation means loving the Creator.

The Golden Rule

But what is love? What is the content of the concept and what are its consequences in everyday life? These are the central questions in this chapter. We get an idea of what neighborly love should be in the "golden rule" given by Jesus: "In everything do to others as you would have them do to you; for this is the law and the prophets"

(Matt 7:12). We normally have no problem in wishing the best for ourselves; and Jesus wants us to expand that self-love to others, to cross the boundaries that we set up between ourselves and our neighbors, to practice the harmonious existence created by an inclusive love. But I have heard of a "platinum rule" added to the golden rule; the platinum rule demands that you wish for others the best as they see it, not as what you deem the best for them. The platinum rule makes a lot of sense, for we often try to force our will on others, thinking that they should wish for themselves what we wish for them. If neighborly love entails benevolence to our neighbor as to ourselves, how do we know what is best for them? How should we respond when we think our neighbor is walking on the edge of the abyss, but seems to be happy with the life he leads? How do we even know what is best for ourselves?

Four Loves

When we learn that Jesus regards love as the most important virtue, it does not solve all our ethical problems. We often find it difficult to know what love entails in everyday situations; we can't even give a definition of the word "love," since so many different things have been called "love." The central virtue of Christianity has become cheap; we call each other "dear" and "love" without meaning anything by it.

In his book titled *The Four Loves*, C. S. Lewis distinguishes between various kinds of love. In the introduction he writes about the general contrast between gift-love and need-love. As Christians, we tend to think that our love should be a "pure" gift-love, one that does not think about its own needs, but focuses completely on giving instead of receiving. However, Lewis warns that we as humans are in our essence needy creatures, that "our whole being by its very nature is one big need; incomplete, preparatory, empty yet cluttered, crying out for Him who can untie things that are now knotted together and tie up things that are still dangling loose."[37] We can therefore not get away from the fact that needing and giving are intertwined in love. "Those who come nearest to a Gift-love for God will next moment, even at the very same moment, be beating their breasts with the publican and laying their indigence before the only real Giver."[38] To love therefore means to be willing to give as well as to receive. Another important point that Lewis mentions in the introduction is that our earthly loves can easily become destructive if we idolize them. He warns: "We may give our human loves the unconditional allegiance which we owe only to God: then they become demons."[39] Love is heavenly; but it can also be hellish.

After the introduction Lewis devotes a chapter on love for the subhuman ("I love my early morning coffee"). Then he goes on to discuss the four kinds of love referred to in the title: affection (the love for what has become familiar to us, as Henry Higgins said in *My Fair Lady*: "I've grown accustomed to her face"), friendship, *eros*, and *caritas*. The last mentioned is the Christian virtue of love; it is a love received as a gift from the all-loving God, which enables us "to love what is not naturally lovable; lepers, criminals, enemies, morons, the sulky, the superior and the sneering."[40] Lewis stresses that *caritas* (charity) involves both gift-love and need-love; it is also not dissociated from the human loves of affection, friendship, and *eros* discussed in the previous three chapters—*caritas* becomes incarnated in them, so that the most humble relationships receive a heavenly flavor:

> All the activities (sins only excepted) of the natural loves can in a favored hour become works of the glad and shameless and grateful Need-love or of the selfless, unofficious Gift-love, which are both Charity. Nothing is either

37. Lewis, *Four Loves*, 9
38. Ibid., 9.
39. Ibid., 13.
40. Ibid., 117.

too trivial or too animal to be thus transformed.... Thus in our very instincts, appetites and recreations, Love has prepared for Himself "a body."[41]

Paul's Description of Love

Although there is no all-encompassing definition of love, Paul gives us a thought-provoking description of the qualities of this cardinal virtue: "Love is patient; love is kind; love is not envious or boastful or arrogant or rude. It does not insist on its own way; it is not irritable or resentful; it does not rejoice in wrongdoing, but rejoices in the truth. It bears all things, believes all things, hopes all things, endures all things" (1 Cor 13:4-7).

Perhaps the most fundamental aspect of love is its benevolence—it is kind; it wishes well. The loving person is also patient, knowing that patience is needed during the development of the soul. Furthermore, love takes others into consideration; it does not insist on its own way; it is willing to suffer and endure for the sake of harmonious relations; it hopes and continues to believe in its transforming power. Love is also humble, knowing that boastfulness and arrogance are the antitheses of love; for the proud, self-centered person is blind to the needs of others.

Loving Our Enemy

In the chapter on "Righteousness Etc." I mentioned one unique quality of the Christian faith: the belief in the unconditional grace of God. But the teaching of Jesus contains another element that is quite unique: "You have heard that it was said, 'You shall love your neighbor and hate your enemy.' But I say to you, love your enemies and pray for those who persecute you, so that you may be children of your Father in heaven; for He makes his sun rise on the evil and on the good, and sends rain on the righteous and on the unrighteous" (Matt 5:43-45).

41. Ibid., 122.

Love

The command in Leviticus 19 to which Jesus refers is the command to love your neighbor; the part about hating your enemy was added by the lawyers. Jesus especially criticizes this addition: in contrast to the lawyers, he declares that those who do not belong to Israel should be loved, not hated—even the enemy should be included in the all-encompassing love of his disciples. Connected to this command is Jesus' instruction to forgive all who have trespassed against us; if we forgive unconditionally, God's channel of unconditional forgiveness will be opened for us (Matt 6:14–15). Jesus knows that the vicious cycle of violence and evil cannot be broken by retaliation, but only by love and forgiveness. This view is later echoed by Paul in his letter to the Romans: "Do not be overcome by evil, but overcome evil with good" (Rom 12:21).

Jesus' Reinterpretation of the Law

Without trying to give a definition of love or to prescribe how to be loving in specific circumstances, I want to point out some of the most striking qualities of love as preached and practiced by Jesus. When a lawyer asked him what he should do to inherit eternal life, Jesus gave two linked commands: to love God with your whole heart, and to love your neighbor as yourself. He was quoting from Deuteronomy and Leviticus to reveal the essence of the law of God; but in his life and in his teaching he did not merely repeat the commands, but reinterpreted them.

According to Deuteronomy 6:5, to which Jesus refers, the love of God should result in obedience to the laws as revealed to Moses on the mount of Sinai. The Pharisees were great at obeying the laws to the letter, but missed the heart of it—loving God. Jesus warned his listeners that their righteousness should be greater than that of the Pharisees. He said that he had come not to abolish the law but to fulfill it (Matt 5:17, 20)—fulfill it by revealing its essence. In his life and death he showed that perfect love towards God does not consist of obeying a set of rules, but consists of total commitment to God—a commitment unto death, with nothing held back. In a similar vein, Paul characterizes the Christian life as a daily sacrifice to God, a total dedication that has taken the place of the sacrificial offerings of the previous dispensation: "I appeal to you therefore, brothers and sisters, by the mercies of God, to present your bodies as a living sacrifice, holy and acceptable to God, which is your spiritual worship" (Rom 12:1). This dedication is the appropriate response to the total commitment of God as shown in the sacrifice of Jesus Christ.

The second command that Jesus mentions comes from Leviticus 19:18. Leviticus refers to love towards fellow Israelites, to those who are "your people." The lawyer who asks Jesus about the greatest law would have been aware of Jesus' opposition to Jewish exclusivity. He therefore asks a second question, probably meant to put Jesus in a difficult position, to force him into making a statement that would offend "true" Israelites. "Who is my neighbor?" he asks. Jesus responds, typically, with a story—the story of the good Samaritan. After the story, he asks the lawyer to answer his own question—but he puts the question in a surprising way: "Which of these three, do you think, was a neighbor to the man who fell into the hands of the robbers?" (Luke 10:36). For Jesus the important question is not, "Who is my neighbor?" but rather, "To whom am I a neighbor?" The story makes the answer obvious, and in verse 37 the lawyer answers correctly: "The one who showed him mercy."

In the story there are four characters: a man who fell into the hands of robbers, a priest, a Levite, and a Samaritan. The priest and the Levite, who are supposed to know the law of God, pass the man by—they are familiar with the letter of the law, but blind to a man in desperate need. The Samaritan, a man who belonged to a group that, according to conservative Jews, did not believe "correctly" because they did not worship in the temple in Jerusalem—he acts according to the spirit of the law of God and shows mercy to a man needing his help. Motivated by care for a fellow human being, he crosses the boundaries created by ethnicity, and alleviates the suffering of a wounded "neighbor."

The important point about Jesus' narrative is that nearness is not a physical matter, but one of attitude. The priest and the Levite were in close proximity to the man in need, but inwardly removed from him. Similarly, distance is a question of attitude. We can be distant to those living closest to us—our spouse, our children, or our parents—but we can also, in our hearts, be close to people in faraway countries—we can pray for them, and send aid to those in need. We are the ones who create barriers between ourselves and our neighbors, or break through the barriers keeping us apart.

The Miraculous Feeding of the Crowd

Another striking quality of the love of Jesus is that he cared for the whole person—he did not restrict his salvation to the body or the spirit. In Mark 6 we read how the people kept on following Jesus, even when he tried to reach a lonely place where he and his disciples could rest. When he saw the great crowd gathered, "he had compassion for them, because they were like sheep without a shepherd" (v. 34). Jesus knew that their most fundamental need was a spiritual one; he realized that their lives were without direction or meaning, so he responded to that need and "began to teach them many things." He was aware that, should they follow his teaching, their lives would become meaningful; their relationship with God would be restored; their deepest need would be fulfilled.

The story does not end here, though. It became late, and the people had nothing to eat. The disciples wanted to send them away to buy food, but Jesus gave them a surprising command: "You give them something to eat" (v. 37). The disciples, taken aback, replied that they only had five loaves of bread and two fish among them, indicating that a crowd of thousands could obviously not be fed by that. But then Jesus came with another surprise: "He ordered them to get all the people to sit down in groups on the green grass" (v. 39). After that, he looked up to heaven, broke the bread, and gave it to the disciples to divide among the people; the fish were handed out as well. And all the people were fed, with twelve baskets of leftovers remaining.

Note that Jesus did not tell the people to follow his commands and forget about their empty stomachs—he cared for their spiritual as well as their physical hunger. Before he handed out the food, he thanked God, acknowledging that all gifts come from above, the physical as well as the spiritual. He knew that God was on the point of performing a miracle, and praised God for it—the miracle of providing nourishment for so many people with so little food. Furthermore, we should note that Jesus did not personally hand out all the food to the people, but used the disciples to distribute it. In other words, they became the channels of God's provision; the miracle happened through their hands. In the world of today, with such sharp divisions between rich and poor, this miracle has a special relevance. We need another multiplication of bread, happening through the hands of Jesus' disciples, so that the abundance of the rich will be shared with the poor, and the undernourished will be fed. It will have to begin with a miraculous change of heart in those who have more than enough.

But there are other facets to this story as well. Mark mentions that the grass was green (Mark 6:39)—so it was springtime, the time of Passover. In the Gospel of John 6:4 it is specifically mentioned that Passover was near. John, always sensitive to the spiritual side of happenings, communicates the symbolic meaning of the event in the rest of the chapter. Jesus warned the people who came to him the next day, keen to be fed once more, that they should not focus exclusively on physical food and neglect the food providing eternal life (vv. 26–27). In the subsequent discussion he compares himself to the manna, the bread from heaven that fed the Israelites in the desert, and tells them what is necessary to attain eternal life: not to perform a difficult task, but to believe in him whom God sent to the earth (v. 29). And then he says explicitly: "I am the bread of life. Whoever comes to me will never be hungry, and whoever comes to me will never be thirsty" (v. 35). So the miraculous provision of food for the crowd prefigures another miracle, the miracle of Golgotha, more glorious than the first—the miracle of providing food for the deepest hunger of the human race. As with the feeding of the crowd, the disciples were involved in the miracle of salvation; they were commanded, after the resurrection, to distribute the eternal bread to the starving multitudes. That would be their gift of love to the world.

Three aspects of the loving care of Jesus can be extracted from the miracle of the feeding of the crowds as we read about it in the Gospel of Matthew: (1) he spoke to the people's spiritual hunger, telling them about the values and conditions of the kingdom of God, which formed the core of his teaching; (2) he gave bread and fish to the hungry crowd, thus attending to their bodily needs; (3) he sacrificed himself to become the bread of life, providing grace and forgiveness to sinners unable to conform to the high standards of the kingdom of heaven.

The Salt of the Earth

We are called to establish the kingdom of God on earth. However, looking around us and reading history, we are confronted with the fact that the kingdom of God has never been completely established on earth. The secular world tends to follow its own self-centered norms. What should the Christian's role be in a world that seems to be rebelling against the reign of God?

An image used by Jesus also suggests that his followers would be in the minority: he told them that they were the salt of the earth (Matt 5:13). We only use a little bit of salt in food; and indeed, the disciples following Jesus, taking up his cross, and following his commands would be, comparatively speaking, only a few. Salt has two functions: it gives taste to food and acts as a preserver. A little bit of salt, a small dose of self-sacrificing love, gives flavor to the world around it and keeps it from rotting. For if all people followed their selfish desires, if no one was prepared to spread love around him, the world would indeed go to rot—or, to use another image of Jesus, darkness would reign completely (compare Matt 5:14).

A little bit of salt can spread its flavor until it changes the taste of all the food to which it is added; it "sacrifices" its separate taste to make the surrounding food flavorsome. The spreading of the flavor starts from where the salt is; it changes the immediate environment first and gradually spreads further and further until all the food is reached and the taste of the salt is integrated with its surroundings. The process is similar to that referred to in another image that Christ used—that of the yeast: "The kingdom of heaven is like yeast that a woman took and mixed in with three measures of flour until all of it was leavened" (Matt 13:33). The kingdom of heaven, the reign of God established in a person, spreads its influence gradually. Its immediate surroundings are changed first, which in turn transforms the surroundings, and so forth, in a never-ending process. Our influence only reaches a limited number of people, but it does not stop there—they have an influence on others, and from them it spreads further and further. We have a greater influence on the world than we imagine. (Of course, the never-ending spreading is characteristic of the influence of evil as well; so we have the infectious disease of evil competing with the infectious health of goodness—a battle that will continue until the end of the world.)

Exodus 20 tells us how God gave the Ten Commandments to Moses on Sinai, how the people of Israel were afraid when they heard the thunder and saw the lightning and the smoke on the mountain, how they asked Moses if they could remain at a distance while he went up the mountain to speak to God (vv. 18–21). Moses was accepted into God's presence, but the Israelites were afraid that they would die if they should follow their leader. So we find Moses, the holy man, in the presence of God; the priests and leaders of the nation, specifically mentioned in the story, are at a greater distance, but probably not as far away as the frightened crowd of ordinary Israelites. Absent in the story, outside the boundaries of the narrative, are the heathen nations, ignorant of what was happening—but eventually they too would be touched by the story.

Jesus is the Moses of the New Testament, the mediator between God and the people, the one who lived in a closer union with God than we dare to do. From God the message of redemption came to Jesus; from him it spread to his disciples first; and from them always further and further, reaching a great number of new disciples. Not all of them live equally close to God, just as the Israelites were also at different distances from Sinai; but they were all touched by Jesus' message of redemption. Their function, from the most famous to the most humble, is to be the salt of the earth mentioned by Jesus. Each of them who is true to his calling has a beneficial influence on his surroundings—not necessarily by converting many to his faith, but by practicing the virtue of love, which can be infectious; thus letting God's kingdom of love come on earth, in accordance with the prayer of Jesus. But if there is too little salt for a big world—or worse still, if the salt should become tasteless—the rot sets in.

The Changing Colors of Love

The Christian concept of love is full of paradoxes and contrasts; it continually changes its color and looks different in each situation. Love is soft and tender, but can also be as hard as nails; it yields but also stands firm; it is submissive as well as rebellious; sometimes active, sometimes passive—waiting instead of doing. Love accepts others as they are, but is also saddened by their obnoxious qualities; it is appreciative but also critical; patient, but also impatient for the truth to break through. It has a vertical as well as a horizontal dimension; love wishes the best for oneself but also for others; it is characterized by receiving as well as by giving; it is the sign of holiness and also of brokenness. And so one can go on about the contrasts and paradoxes of love.

I love to quote a statement made by Bernard Bosanquet: "When the Absolute falls into the water, it becomes a fish."[42] God, who is absolute, who has no beginning or end, who is timeless and unchanging, is miraculously revealed in our world determined by space and time. God's love is constantly shaped by the situations in which it operates; it provides in various ways. Fish don't walk on the water, but they know how to live from the abundant generosity of the sea. Each created thing fits into and adapts to its evolving environment, and in that environment reveals the wisdom and generosity of its Creator.

The love of God in which Christians believe is absolute and unchanging, but also relative to the situations in which it acts. To follow the line of Bosanquet's argument further: when the

---

42. See Hoernlé, *Idealism*, 176.

Absolute falls into the air, it becomes a bird, free to fly through the air, revealing the power and freedom of the Creator. Something similar yet fundamentally different happened with God's incarnation in Jesus—when the Absolute fell into the human domain, it became Jesus Christ, the perfect human. So much more of God's Person was revealed in the bodily life of Jesus than in the qualities of fish and birds. The essence of God's Being was made known to us in an earthly history that could make sense to us, earthly beings. God's love was revealed in a story of love, performing within the context of human need. God also granted humans the possibility to become imitators of Jesus, showing and spreading God's love on earth. The narrative of the incarnation reveals the wondrous humility of God, which made it possible for us to comprehend and share in some of God's glory.

The Absolute love of God, incarnated in humans, takes on a different form in each situation. It can, at different times, reveal any of its variety of qualities mentioned above. The great challenge for us is to know when we have to act and when we must wait, when we must be hard and when soft, and so forth. Wisdom begins by waiting upon God, being sensitive to the voice of God's Spirit in us, asking God to free us from our anxieties and personal desires, our impetuousness and stubbornness, so that we can make decisions that are right for the situation. For a quality of love shown at the wrong time and place can be hateful. We should not let the fish mentioned by Bosanquet come onto the land, or try to send our lions into the air; love should always take on the form that is appropriate for the situation.

Resisting Evil in Different Ways

It is not always easy to know how to let God's kingdom come on earth. When Dietrich Bonhoeffer landed in prison, he discovered to his surprise how unfamiliar the prisoners were with the gospel in which he believed. If he were to tell them about the vicarious death of Jesus, it would be as incomprehensible to them as if he had spoken in Greek. He therefore came to the conclusion

LOVE

that, under those circumstances, practical deeds of love would be more meaningful than a theological exposition. Similarly, if we as Christians go into the secular world, we should meet people where they are, and not expect them to be where we are. We should follow the example of Paul, who became a Jew to the Jews, and for those outside the law as one outside the law: "I have become all things to all people, that I may by all means save some" (1 Cor 9:22). We should "translate" the Christian doctrine into terms comprehensible for those whom we meet. By our practical deeds of goodness we may attract people to the ethical heart of the gospel, to the virtue of love, without necessarily converting them to the doctrine. We should also be sensitive to the needs of the moment—we should not talk about the atoning death of Christ to a person wanting practical advice from us, or about the resurrection to one complaining of toothache.

Being sensitive to the needs and the convictions of others does not imply that we should conform to the world—salt has to be different to be tasted. Part of the Christian life is to go against the grain; it often deviates from the prescribed norms of the world. This is particularly the case when an evil system reigns in a country. How should a Christian act when evil and corruption are paramount? How can one spread undiscriminating love when it is forbidden by the law? Is violence acceptable to combat an inhuman system? There are many views on these questions, and the conflicting views are all supported by different texts from the Bible. Can there be one final answer to the problem? Ferdinand Deist, in his book *Sê God so?* ("Does God Say So?"), refers to the time of Hitler to give his views on these issues. When the Nazis planned the extinction of the Jews, what would have been the appropriate response for Christians? Deist outlines three kinds of resistance that occurred:

(1) Dietrich Bonhoeffer used the example of a driver driving recklessly—in such a case, one should inform the police. But what if the police don't care? What if the political and judicial systems are corrupt? Then someone has to intervene, he thought—one has to forcefully grab the steering wheel from the driver's hands and steer the car

in the right direction, to prevent innocent people from being killed. For him, Christian love means uncompromising resistance; when the evil power does not want to listen to reason, violence is the only way out. The reign of Hitler was killing millions of people; killing a few was better than having millions killed. So Bonhoeffer decided to join the underground resistance, and he was caught and executed.

(2) Other members of the Confessional Church to which Bonhoeffer belonged—people who were also totally opposed to the policy of Hitler and to the Lutheran Church's connivance with the tyrant—did not want to have recourse to violence. They felt that there were many texts in the New Testament warning against responding to violence with violence, to answering aggression with aggression. So they decided on non-violent protest; they were ostracized and suffered in various ways.

(3) But there were also committed Christians who fought on Hitler's side. Deist mentions the example of a German camp commander who did all in his power to make life as bearable as possible for the Jews in his camp. The inhabitants of the camp appreciated his goodwill so much that they hid him after the war to protect him from retaliation by the Allies.

Which of the three methods of resistance was the right one? Deist does not single out one of the three—these were three possible methods of resisting evil, and all did some good. Bonhoeffer and the members of the Confessional Church saved the message of redemption from losing all credibility; they showed that there were other possibilities for Christians than conniving with evil. The kind Nazi officer showed that good and evil do not coincide with ethnic differences, that love can take on a variety of forms. The important point is to resist evil—the most appropriate method will vary from situation to situation, and from person to person. Love continually changes its color.

In One Word: Love

So far in this chapter we have learned something about the nature and the deeds of love—but the paradoxes and uncertainties have remained. We cannot completely comprehend what love is, though it touches us to the core. All the previous chapters have been about love—they attempted from various perspectives to understand more of its mystery. Explicitly or implicitly, the discussions circled around the love of God as shown in Jesus Christ, and the appropriate human response to God's love. In some way all the chapters are linked to the text with which this chapter starts—about the love of God that we have come to know in Jesus, and the call to live according to the love of God.

We saw in the chapter on "Faith" that there is an abundance of God's grace—the most amazing aspect of God's love—available for us; we don't have to earn God's favor. In the chapter on "Hope" we saw that the Christian's hope is based on trust in our God, whose love was revealed to us through Jesus Christ; the chapter on "Truth" also dealt with the faithfulness of God and the truth of God's love. "Righteousness," we saw, is the foundation of all ethical thinking—to consider conflicting claims fairly and in a spirit of charity to all. Dealing with "Humility," we pondered on the humility of Jesus, the love that drove him to die on the cross—challenging us to follow his example in some small way and be like grains of wheat that fall on the ground, die, and bear fruit. Our peace, we concluded in the chapter on "Joy," is based on surrendering our lives to God, trusting God to work out his benevolent will for us. A central theme in this book is the good news of the Bible as revealed through Jesus: that we have a loving and lovable God. God's faithfulness was shown in the death of Jesus, God's power in the resurrection; God is the ultimate source of our hope and peace. God can be trusted; God is worthy to be praised through our words and deeds. In response to God's original love, we should be filled with love; it should flow from our grateful hearts, back to God and into the world.

Words like "faith," "humility," "joy," and "truth" could be regarded as different names for the word "love"; each reveals a different aspect of the complexity of love. In the previous chapters we have repeatedly discovered how closely connected these discussed concepts are—faith to hope, truth to joy, and all of them linked to love. Often an ethical concept is discussed with another concept not mentioned in the title—righteousness with grace, truth with freedom. One could use any of these concepts as an avenue to explore the richness of Christian ethics; for each virtue would inevitably lead to the others. One should therefore not regard these concepts as disconnected entities, each with an independent existence. Rather, they are all pointers to the same ultimate reality—the reality of God. Their connectedness suggests the unity, the wholeness of God, who wants to make us whole as well.

The glory of God was revealed in Jesus—the incarnation of Love. Christians cannot separate ethics from Jesus, or Jesus from God. Jesus "is the reflection of God's glory and the exact imprint of God's very being" (Heb 1:3). For Christians, ethical thinking does not begin with us, but is a response to God's revelation in Jesus, disclosing who God is and what God expects from us. All the virtues discussed in the preceding chapters are ultimately connected to the good God in whom Christians believe—the God who was revealed in the goodness of Jesus, the God who is Love. Of course, ethical thinking is not restricted to Christians, but this book is not about ethics in general, but about the unique content of Christian ethics.

The ethics of the Bible can be summarized in one word: love. Love became flesh in the person of Jesus—in the narrative of his life, his teachings, his death and his resurrection. Jesus was the "Word of God" (John 1:1). Words are used to communicate; a word is part of a system of communication. The person of Jesus was a richly significant Word from God, revealing to humans the loving heart of God and the way to salvation. We can find much joy in the one Word—but there is a whole language of God that will only be revealed in the life hereafter, when we shall meet God face to face.

Bibliography

Alves, Rubem. *Tomorrow's Child: Imagination, Creativity, and the Rebirth of Culture*. Eugene, OR: Wipf and Stock, 2011.
Armstrong, Karen. *The Case for God*. London: Vintage, 2010.
Bock, Jerry, and Sheldon Harnick. "If I Were a Rich Man." *Fiddler on the Roof*. 1964. https://www.stlyrics.com/lyrics/fiddlerontheroof/ifiwerearichman.htm.
Bonhoeffer, Dietrich. *The Cost of Discipleship*. New York: Simon & Schuster, 1995.
Brother Lawrence, and Frank Laubach. *Practicing His Presence*. Beaumont, TX: SeedSowers, 1995.
Calvin, John. *Institutes of the Christian Religion*. Translated by Henry Beveridge. Peabody, MA: Hendrickson, 2007.
Dante Alighieri. *The Divine Comedy*. In *The Portable Dante*. Translated by Mark Musa. New York: Penguin, 2003.
Deist, Ferdinand. *Sê God so?: Protes en pleidooi oor óns tyd, vir óns land*. Cape Town: Tafelberg, 1982.
Elsschot, Willem. *Kaas*. Amsterdam: Querido, 1933.
Farley, Wendy. *Tragic Vision and Divine Compassion: A Contemporary Theodicy*. Louisville: Westminster/John Knox, 1990.
Foster, Richard J. *Prayer: Finding the Heart's True Home*. London: Hodder & Stoughton, 2008.
Hoernlé, R. F. A. *Idealism as a Philosophical Doctrine*. London: Hodder & Stoughton, 1924.
Kolodiejchuk, Brian, ed. *Mother Teresa: Come Be My Light*. London: Ebury, 2008.
Levi, Primo. *If This Is a Man / The Truce*. Translated by Stuart Woolf. London: Little, Brown, 1988.
Lewis, C. S. *The Four Loves*. New York: HarperCollins, 2012.
———. *Mere Christianity*. New York: HarperCollins, 2012.
Makgoba, Thabo. "Moral Leadership and the Task of Education for the 21st Century" Inaugural lecture as chancellor, University of the Western

BIBLIOGRAPHY

Cape, 28 February 2012. http://www.anglicanaids.net/2012/03/02/archbishop-thabo-makgoba-inaugurated-as-chancellor-of-the-university-of-the-western-cape/

Murray, Andrew. *Humility*. Florida: Bottom of the Hill, 2010.

Pascal, Blaise. *Pensées and other Writings*. Translated by Honor Levi. Oxford: Oxford University Press, 1995.

Robinson, Marilynne. "Marguerite de Navarre." In *The Death of Adam: Essays on Modern Thought*, 174–206. New York: Picador, 2007.

Smit, Dirkie. "Geestelike waardes." *Die Burger*, 31 October 2009, 10.

———. *Neem, lees!: Hoe ons die Bybel hoor en verstaan*. Wellington, South Africa: Lux Verbi, 2006.

Studdert Kennedy, G. A. "The Suffering God." In *The Unutterable Beauty: The Collected Poems of G. A. Studdert Kennedy*, 13–14. Cambridge, UK: Lutterworth, 2008.

Tillich, Paul. "The Escape from God." Sermon, date unknown. http://www.godweb.org/shaking.htm.

Totius [Jacob Daniël du Toit]. "The Earth Is Not Our Dwelling Place." In *Afrikaans Poems with English Translations*, edited by A. P. Grové and C. J. D. Harvey, 24. Cape Town: Oxford University Press, 1962.

Van Melle, J. "Oom Diederik leer om te huil." In *Keur uit die verhale van J. van Melle*, 23–32. Pretoria: J. L. van Schaik, 1964.

Versfeld, Marthinus. *Our Selves*. Pretoria: Protea Boekhuis, 2010.

Wiesel, Elie. *Night*. London: Penguin, 2008.

Wilson, A. N. "Religion of Hatred: Why We Should No Longer Be Cowed by the Chattering Classes Ruling Britain Who Sneer at Christianity." *Daily Mail*, 10 April 2009. http://www.dailymail.co.uk/news/article-1169145/Religion-hatred-Why-longer-cowed-secular-zealots.html.

Yancey, Philip. *What's So Amazing about Grace?* Michigan: Zondervan, 2002.

www.ingramcontent.com/pod-product-compliance
Lightning Source LLC
Chambersburg PA
CBHW071443160426
43195CB00013B/2020